Bringing Up Children Overseas

Other Books by Dr. Sidney Werkman

The Role of Psychiatry in Medical Education

Only a Little Time

BRINGING UP CHILDREN OVERSEAS

A Guide for Families

SIDNEY WERKMAN, M.D.

Basic Books, Inc., Publishers   New York

I would like to thank the editors of *Foreign Service Journal* for permission to reprint my article titled "Over Here and Back There: American Adolescents Overseas," which appeared in their March 1975 issue.

Excerpt from "The Love Song of J. Alfred Prufrock" in *Collected Poems 1909–1962* by T. S. Eliot, copyright, © 1936, by Harcourt Brace Jovanovich, Inc.; copyright, © 1963, 1964, by T. S. Eliot. Reprinted by permission of the publishers.

649.1
Werkman, Sidney

Library of Congress Cataloging in Publication Data

Werkman, Sidney
  Bringing up children overseas.

  Includes index.
  1. Children of military personnel. 2. Children—Management. 3. United States—Armed Forces—Foreign countries. I. Title
U766.W418   649'.1   76-43490
ISBN: 0-465-00759-7

Demondoten – 7-11-77 – 9.95

CONTENTS

Contents

PREFACE

"The wildest dreams of Kew are the facts of Katmandu," wrote Kipling. This book, however, is about the hard facts of overseas life, not the dreams; the stresses rather than the adventures. If an American family moves to Tunisia, for example, it is important to plan for more than dinner parties and weekends of bright sun at Sidi Bou Said. Many hours will be consumed in dealing with household help and puzzling over children who substitute Tunisian-French values for stateside ways. One cannot fashion a satisfactory life in London solely by visits to cultural and historical sites. Other issues will take precedence. For example, wives must feel secure that their abilities are respected, and children need to know that their parents care about them.

From the wide range of topics presented in these pages, focus on those that speak to your particular situation. First-timers may wish to turn to the many incidents quoted from hundreds of interviews with overseas people in order to get an overview of what is ahead. Old hands may be more concerned with specific questions about teenagers, women's careers, or when and how to return to the United States. The examples that I use and the conclusions that I reach are meant to stimulate a traveler's thinking and provide alternate points of view for making decisions, not to suggest that there is only one right way to do things.

Obviously, it is impossible to portray each situation a family will face or to depict every local condition to be found throughout the world. After all, "East is East and West is West" in life as well as in Kipling. Schools vary from country to country; caretakers are not available in some places; the lives of military families in Brussels differ from those in Frankfurt. However, all families will have more satisfactory experiences if they learn to cope effectively with the inevitable tasks of preparing, moving, settling in, raising children in a new environment and, finally, returning to the United States.

A willingness to confront these tasks directly can make international life infinitely easier, for, as a woman who has lived overseas for many years observed to me, "The single most pervasive problem for overseas families is the denial, particularly by fathers, that any special family problems exist." I can assure the reader, from the vantage point of psychiatric practice in Washington, consultant work with the State Department and Peace Corps, as well as my own experience in living away from the United States, that special family problems *do* exist for overseas people.

Though the title focuses on children, *Bringing Up Children Overseas* really is about families. Those of us who work with children recognize increasingly that individual decisions crucially effect the development and mental health of each member of a family; no family member's needs can be understood in isolation. As family members overseas are thrown into unusually intimate contact with each other, the principle of shared decision making becomes singularly important for them.

Much of the book concentrates on the art and techniques of successful transitions, for competence in dealing with change effectively is the single most important ability for Americans who move around the world to master. No matter how well a person speaks French or understands world history, such accomplishments will offer small comfort if family conflicts or the ways of host-country people create chronic upset. Whether one is going overseas for the first time or a fifth time, planning and forethought are the keys to success.

This book is about those keys.

ACKNOWLEDGMENTS

As this book developed from interviews with American families in Europe, Asia, and Africa, and from seminars at the Foreign Service Institute and the Business Council for International Understanding, I wish to express my warm appreciation to the hundreds of children, parents, teachers, school administrators, and international executives who contributed their time, ideas, and warm support to the project. For their valuable comments on sections of the manuscript I am most grateful to: Dr. Frank Johnson, Psychiatrist, Medical Division, Department of State; Drs. Paul Luebke and Gordon Parsons, Division of Overseas Schools, Department of State; Dr. Anthony Cardinale, Director, Office of Overseas Dependents Education, Department of Defense; Colonel Roy Prince, Colonel Lawrence Isom, and Major Ronald Raybin, U.S. Army Medical Corps. Mrs. Shirley Newhall, editor of the *Foreign Service Journal*, gave much appreciated advice and encouragement.

My special thanks go to the following colleagues at the University of Colorado School of Medicine who made penetrating observations and suggestions: Drs. Gaston Blom, John Cobb, Peter Dawson, Dane Prugh, Scott Robertson, Rhoda Singer, and Michael Solomon.

Of the many overseas hands who offered ideas and read portions of the book, I would like to acknowledge the particular contributions of Mrs. John Cobb, Mrs. Lee Dane, Mr. Peter Dominick Jr., Mrs. Alfred Friendly, Mrs. Nicholas Platt, Mrs. Caroline Service and Mr. & Mrs. Richard Wagner. Mrs. Virginia McGehee, Mrs. Mary McPhee, and Mr. Curtis

Casewit offered expert editorial service. Mrs. Nancy McGee did excellent work in typing the manuscript.

Though the book reflects the experiences and opinions of countless international experts and overseas families, I happily take responsibility for the conclusions expressed. My wife, an unwitting experimental subject in this study, can ably state her own views about the validity of the book's conclusions. I can merely express my love and appreciation to her for allowing it to be written during a time of transition.

Because better forms have not yet been invented, the text utilizes the conventional words "he" and "him" to encompass both male and female roles—though with apologies to my two daughters, as well as all other girls and women.

Bringing Up Children Overseas

"Chance favors the prepared mind."
—Louis Pasteur

I

What Is It Like Over There?

ASURVEY I conducted with people overseas revealed that most had similar questions on their minds at particular stages of their careers. This chapter offers a sample of the questions reported most frequently in the survey, followed by my own observations, which are offered to help the reader focus his own thinking toward personal solutions. The questions and the answers given are not meant to provide definitive guidance, because many of the big issues cannot be settled by simple, universally applicable conclusions. Instead, the chapter can be read as an overview of typical family problems and a way of approaching solutions to them. Subsequent chapters referred to cover all the issues in greater detail.

"Are the schools good?" All parents who plan to move overseas worry over this question. Those Americans who are already overseas turn it into, "Can my child get as good an edu-

cation here as he would in the United States?" Fortunately, the answer to both questions is "yes."

The network of 500 schools throughout the world sponsored by the Department of Defense, the Office of Overseas Schools of the State Department, and International Schools Services, as well as missionary schools and privately funded schools, offer educational opportunities equal to, and in many cases far superior to, those available to most children in the United States.

Children who attend these schools make up a select group whose parents are enterprising and educationally oriented; overseas teachers have chosen to work in their particular country. Many of the schools radiate an atmosphere of intimacy and concern for the individuality of each student that is no longer available in typical schools in the United States. The majority of children from overseas schools score as well as or better than their peers on achievement tests when they return to the United States.

However, the special child—the dedicated young scientist, the fanatical football player, the budding actor, or the devoted ballet dancer—may not find the teachers, coaches, sophisticated laboratories, and companions they wish. A child with extremely specialized interests might be disappointed overseas; he may have to give up a particular hobby or choose an alternate one. But all educational decisions should weigh possible deficiencies in particular courses or extracurricular activities against the brillant artistic, cultural, and geographical experiences available to any child who has the chance to live abroad (chap. 9).

"My wife is dragging her feet about moving to England, and I am afraid that when we go overseas (for the first time) she will come apart. She is a shy person, very close to her mother, who lives near us, and sort of unadventuresome. How can I help her?"

What Is It Like Over There?

Even the healthiest families may contain one member who balks at moving overseas. Still, consider the possibility that your wife is ready to cut the apron strings that tie her to her mother and needs your support in doing so. It may ease her mind to recognize that fear of change is a healthy part of anticipated transition, and that one of the great benefits of a move can be to overcome inhibitions and achieve independence.

Make sure the wish to move is not yours alone but one that she shares. It is certain that a wife who hangs back from moving away from home will push to return home as soon as possible, unless she gets a great deal of support from her husband. Talk with your wife about the whole range of concerns between you, and expect all the family ghosts to come out of the closet, for they will. Perhaps she believes you foster her timidity. Remember that you are part of your wife's problem, just as both spouses are involved when one is alcoholic.

If the two of you cannot settle her fears, consider obtaining the professional help of a family counselor skilled in dealing with decisions about life's transitions. With such assistance, the cause of your wife's anxiety can be examined and resolved for good and all, before a move is made. Sensitive concern— not giving in to her fears or, on the other hand, forcing the move—is the treatment needed (chaps. 4, 7, 8).

"I have been offered a fine job with my company overseas. It means a lot to my career to take the post, but my son will enter his senior year in high school in Washington next September. Will it do him harm to be taken out of high school?"

Experts unanimously offer the same answer to this dilemma. They suggest *not* to take teenagers out of high school and move them overseas, unless no alternative exists. The social network of an American high school is a rigid one, hard to leave and very difficult to reenter. The senior year in high school is the important one for teenagers. It is the culmination of all their efforts to make friends, join teams, and lead activities. Few young people want to leave home with such rewards in sight.

As one father put it, "I was offered an overseas job that would have advanced my professional career, but it would have taken my son away from his friends, his activities, and being captain of the basketball team. I had to decide between my career and my son. I am proud that I decided in my son's favor, and I have never been sorry for doing it" (chaps. 10, 14).

"We moved to France just when our 15-year-old daughter was becoming a leader of her group in junior high school and was in line to become a cheerleader. Here in Paris she talks about nothing but home. She just won't work and is constantly surly to her mother and me. What can we do?"

Teenagers deserve to participate in family decisions about a move. If a daughter feels she was whisked away from the United States without being consulted, the remedy is to talk frankly with her now, even though she cannot be taken back to the United States for the moment. Admit past errors. An adult may speak frankly of the present and see what can be retrieved. Possibly, she needs a chance to grieve, to express her feelings about separation and loss. She should be given this chance without the burden of your further comments or disagreements. You can help your daughter pursue interesting activities in France, for, after feelings have been recognized and openly expressed, the best way to get beyond regret is through involvement (chaps. 4, 7, 10, 13).

"We have been in Brussels for five years. Our company now wants us to move to another country in Europe or return to the United States. How can we decide what to do?"

A second, lateral move overseas usually results in a long-term commitment to international life, or, at times, a big disappointment. People who remain away from the United States many years tend to lose contact with current trends in business, a profession, or life here in general. The more time an American spends overseas, the less sensitive he will be to many aspects of his own country. Decide whether your particular career ambitions and your family's needs can best be served by staying away from the United States for a longer period of time. It will be worthwhile to list the negatives as well as the positives before making a decision. After glorious first tours, many people neglect to consider whether a second one will be as satisfactory, just as a child who has enjoyed one large bowl of ice cream plunges into another without thinking of the consequences.

Children often become the crucial factor in a decision about whether to remain overseas, and they should come first in an adult's calculations. Young children adapt well to lateral moves, but teenagers often become the focus for trouble. "We came back because of our sixteen-year-old," is a frequent statement made by returned Americans. Teenagers who have lived overseas all of their lives are content to remain away from the United States until college; those who have lived away only a few years, and still cherish the memories of close friends and social activities at home, may force a parent's hand about returning to America. It is unwise to "scapegoat" a child, placing the complete burden of a decision to return on the needs of a teenager, if, in reality, that decision rests on other personal or career concerns (chaps. 4, 6, 10, 14).

"I just got my orders to go to an Army post near Frankfurt for a two-year assignment. Should I take my wife and children or leave them at home?"

The critical decisions for military families concern the education of children, family housing, and economics. At all times, the most crucial questions have to do with the welfare of the children; after all, the family is the caretaker of the child. Parents must therefore ask themselves, "Are the living arrangements adequate? Will the children have their own room? enough privacy? Is good schooling available? Will the new post offer ample baby-sitting or other child care, tutoring (if necessary), and other assistance for slow learners? Will there be provisions for a possibly handicapped American child?"

The financial side of such a move should be anticipated as well. A balance sheet can be worked out in writing. In the case of a short-term move, Americans sometimes prefer to leave their offspring with relatives; if parents contemplate such a measure, they must also ponder the possible difficulties while they are abroad.

It is important to emphasize that a decision should include the views of *all* family members. Adults must also privately discuss their own position toward one another and toward their children and avoid the tendency to "escape" overseas to evade pressing family concerns. A father's ailing relationship with a daughter, for instance, could be aggravated by a long absence. And travel *sans* children would complicate an already cool relationship between mother and son.

Family problems may be postponed if a husband opts for an unaccompanied tour overseas, but those problems merely fester and emerge in a more serious form at a later time. Families who want to remain together usually find a way to travel together (chap. 11).

"What about languages? Our two-year-old is learning Thai from a caretaker, and he seems to understand that better than he does English."

The natural curiosity and mimicking abilities of young children are easily harnessed into the learning of two languages at once, and with no harm done. Research studies confirm that most young children can become fluent in several languages and are unaware of the magnitude of their accomplishment. The child who spends most of his time with a caretaker will speak her language and pick up her accent. The language to worry about is English and not that of the host country. A child should spend enough time with his parents to maintain the English language.

8

What Is It Like Over There?

Sometimes parents who do not speak the host country tongue nevertheless try to inflict language training on their children. Such attempts can end in disaster. If you want your child to learn a second language, study that language yourself and use it at home (chaps. 7, 9).

"We live on an Army post in the Middle East where facilities for high-school-age children are not adequate. Should I send my 15-year-old daughter to a military-sponsored boarding school in England? What preparations will she need before going to a boarding school?"

You may feel uncomfortable at first with the thought of sending your youngster away to school; many parents initially react to the idea as one foreign to the American way of life. However, boarding schools do form a natural part of the overseas experience for Americans, and teenagers from all walks of life have attended international boarding schools, emerging as fine, able adults. If you are not acquainted with such institutions, visits to several of them will pay dividends far beyond the cost of travel. The Office of Overseas Schools of the Department of State or the Porter Sargent Directory listed in chapter 9 will steer you to appropriate boarding schools in your area.

Some military families believe, mistakenly, that their children must attend military-sponsored schools. Many top-notch civilian boarding facilities exist throughout Europe and in other parts of the world. The costs vary, depending upon the country, from $2,000 to $3,500 per year, but the current average is approximately $3,000 per year. Although private schooling adds to the expense of education, the results justify the extra cost. If a military dependents' school is not available in your area, the military service will pay the entire cost of tuition at a boarding school for your child. In some cases, the cost of correspondence courses will be paid for by the military services. Army Community Services and Air Force Family Services counselors at your post can help you apply for financial aid in support of your childrens' education.

If you decide to send your daughter to a boarding school, be sure to discuss thoroughly what it will mean for her to live away from you. Assure yourself that she is independent enough to study on her own and reach out to make friends comfortably. If not, a crash course in study habits and assertiveness may be useful before she leaves home.

Choose a school that states its study hour requirements clearly; look for one that plans ample, well-structured weekend activities, for weekends can be the most disturbing times for teenagers away from home. Be certain that you understand the behavioral code of the school and that you agree with it.

Boarding-school teachers cannot take over the parenting of a child. It is vital to keep in contact with a teenager via a regular, two-way correspondence agreed to as part of the bargain when she (or he) leaves for boarding school. Occasional telephone calls and visits are important, too. Establish regular communication with an identified educator, counselor, or school official; teachers can do more for their students when parents show a continuing interest in the educational process (chaps. 9, 10, 11).

"My seven-year-old, who was born here in the Philippines, has had an aya *(caretaker) her entire life. We are returning to the United States in several months, and I wonder whether we should tell her we are going to leave the* aya *behind or just go about the business of packing and down-play the whole thing. We even considered bringing the* aya *with us. Mainly, how do we leave without causing the child pain?"*

It can't be done. A separation inevitably brings some sorrow, for young children become almost as closely attached to caretakers as to their mothers.

If a parent must separate a child from her *aya*, a talk with both of them about the change well in advance of moving day—perhaps a month or so—proves helpful. Encourage them to express their feelings, together and with you. An attempt to hide the reality of the separation may confuse a child and cause her to lose confidence in her parents.

Do not bring your caretaker all the way to the United States if the sole motivation is to decrease your child's sense of loss, for endless complications may ensue. A child will soon no longer need her *aya* yet may feel obligated to her; the caretaker may have great difficulty in adjusting to the United States; and the adult may not have worked through the feelings of loss that initiated the whole operation (chaps. 8, 14).

"Our eighteen-year-old, who has spent the last ten years in Latin America, plans to return to college in the United States next year. How can she decide what college to attend? How can we prepare for her return to the United States?"

Talk with the counselor in her high school; write away for college catalogs; ask for advice by mail from a college placement counselor in a high school in your home town. The State Department and the military services employ school counselors; perhaps your organization has one.

If at all feasible, a parent should make a special trip to the United States with the teenager to visit colleges. This will provide opportunities to make contact with other college-bound youngsters and test the atmosphere of different universities. Fortunately, college admissions officers value international experience highly, as they should, and overseas youngsters with adequate high-school records are highly respected.

Since your daughter has been away from the United States a good while, she may be out of date with clothing styles, the ways young people relate to one another, and the whole tempo of life in the U.S. Most returning teenagers agree that, as one person put it, "The real trouble in coming back is not academic, it's social" (chaps. 10, 14).

Whereas generally applicable solutions fit some questions, others require thought that reaches into the depths of the individual experience of a particular person and his family. And

11

even unique problems contain basic concerns common to all. Here are some of the big questions shared by many families:

"How can a woman live a fulfilling life overseas?"

"Are there any special strains on a marriage?"

"How can we avoid the occupational hazards of heavy social drinking and the family disruptions of a demanding social schedule?"

"How will living overseas change my child?"

"Will my child be able to return to the United States and become a real "American" or will he be seen as some kind of freak?"

Future chapters examine these and many more questions in depth. For each question, principles basic to good adjustment should be in the forefront of your mind as you seek the answers that fit your family. Difficult problems have never yielded to facile solutions, but the family that confronts problems directly is bound to hit on better answers than the one that turns away from them.

"Why do I want to live overseas?" is a prime question for anyone committed to an international life. It is an issue to ponder at any stage in a career, and different answers will emerge at different times. The next chapter examines this bedrock issue and offers examples of ways in which others have probed for answers.

II

"For always roaming with a hungry heart.
Much have I seen and known. . . ."
—Tennyson

The Lure of Living Overseas

W HY DID I leave the United States?" "What am I searching for?" "Why did I come here?" Even partial solutions to such deep questions help make life more coherent. The case is simple enough for those who choose a career in the military or in the Foreign Service. Others who live away from the United States may have to dig more deeply to discover their basic motives. For all, the search for answers can pay off handsomely in peace of mind and effectiveness. There are many possible motivations for working overseas. A United Nations official spoke for many overseas Americans when he told me: "From the time I was twelve years old I was interested in reading history and what I later learned to be political science. A biography of Metternich set me off. I never wanted to be involved in anything else but diplomacy." His wife, who had studied languages in college, shared her husband's vision.

They raised their children with the expectation that changes of language, culture, friends, and schools would become a natural part of their lives.

The story is altogether different for the wife of a Washington, D.C., business executive who explained an overseas move this way: "My husband, just out of college, wanted to be a history teacher. He had a hard time finding a teaching job. He wound up working part time for a newspaper while he waited for an opening. When a friend told him about this corporation, it sounded nice, even though we weren't sure that we wanted to live in Arabia. Neither my husband nor I had ever been this far away, but we thought it would be fun. The people would be different. Learning a new language would be adventurous and intriguing, and the government would be enlightening to observe." In brief, this family went overseas only by accident but with the right attitudes.

"It beats me to figure out what got me here to Karachi," a businessman told me candidly. "Maybe it was the *National Geographic* magazines. I grew up in Ohio. My father thought that driving to Cleveland was a big deal! But my mother was never happy in Ohio. Her parents had been missionaries in China, and she lived there when she was a little girl. Always talked about it, too. She just blossomed when she spoke about those days. I guess I caught the bug from her."

Many people harbor secret dreams for a life of greater excitement and fulfillment than the one they lead. The Francophiles and Anglophiles, the people who love another culture, find themselves drawn away from the United States to the art and history of Europe. Some Americans look for less pressure in their careers. They prefer an easier pace than that of the United States. Others, the true exiles, may reject their home country in the belief that they have been rejected by it.

Though reasons for travel form as many patterns as a kaleidoscope, a recurring theme seems to play through the lives of people who choose to move away from the United States. The late James R. Ullman, Himalayan climber and expedition diarist, spoke of them as "elsewhere men, people restlessly seeking for new places." Freya Stark, the travel writer, stated it well: "Traveling is a conscious or unconscious searching for something that is lacking in our lives or in ourselves."

Americans who live overseas often are motivated by the need for a different, a better way of life than they found in the United States. When we know what we want, life becomes simpler, for the family that a has a clear idea of its wellsprings will be freed of many of the conflicts that so often disturb adult relationships and perplex children. Some unconscious motivations may be interwoven with more rational ones. One couple, for instance, may hope to open new cultural horizons for their ten-year-old while the father also may count on the profitable "overseas differential." The son gets an introduction to Africa while the father salts away $5,000 from the year abroad. Nor can anyone deny the inherent romance of travel. Mark Twain sang the praises of Venetian gondolas; Henry James enthused about the Americans' European impressions in *The Ambassadors.*

Romance and Adventure

A foreign trip may stir up passionate longings, for travel tends to weaken a person's defenses against the eruption of deeper impulses. Any traveler who notes his idle thoughts will confirm the truth of this observation, which has been adopted enthusiastically by airline companies that dress their stewardesses glamorously and use sexually provocative copy in their advertisements. Airport newsstands filled with erotic magazines and books give further testimony to what may be on some passengers' minds.

Some people become transformed when they leave the United States. The reserved person may turn into a gregarious soul, the inhibited one into a free spirit, oblivious to the constraints of social convention. The use of a different language encourages a sense of freedom and, as an American in Brazil told me, "I know I'm two people. The one who uses English is quiet and precise; the Portuguese one gestures and is poetic and free."

It is not only the Walter Mitty impulse but, possibly, a basic exploratory drive deriving from man's earliest nomadic origins that spurs people toward the challenge of the unknown and the search for fresh scenes. Why else would so many old and dying people subject themselves to the discomforts of travel?

A Wish To Discover a Heritage

The Grand Tour of the eighteenth century gave young Englishmen the opportunity to learn about the manners, food, and art of the continent of Europe. American writers, at least from the time of Henry James to the great exodus of expatriates in the 1920s, streamed to Europe to transform their lives through immersion in an older culture. The wish to find roots—in Ireland, Armenia, Germany, France, Sicily—still remains alive in many Americans.

Escape

A person in the United States who is burdened with family problems or job difficulties often longs to flee—to put thousands of miles between himself and an irreconcilable relationship. When bills lie unpaid, faucets leak, or relatives make difficult demands, who has not daydreamed of an idyllic life in a remote part of the world?

The Hope for Eternal Renewal

The rhythm of repeated moves protects against boredom and a narrowing of career interests. People constantly on the move are freed from observing the illnesses and aging of their friends and colleagues, or looking into themselves. New friends and new challenges always appear on the horizon. For those voyagers, the passage of time is halted. Many observers note that people who live the transient overseas life seem younger than their age mates who remain in the United States.

Irrational Fantasies

In many "elsewhere men," a secret wish lies hidden beneath rational goals. For some it is the hope to recapture the exhilaration of a first love or the mystical feeling of spiritual power they might have known as adolescents. For others, it may be the attempt to flee a painful memory or unresolved guilt. People caught up in such struggles often hope to disenthrall themselves of the past and set their lives on fresh paths through travel.

From the many travelers I have encountered over the years, I have invented, only slightly tongue in cheek, a group of patterns or syndromes to characterize the motivations of Americans who live overseas.

The Maharaja Syndrome

The "Maharaja" hopes to spend his tour sitting on an elephant, while mundane matters are taken care of by underlings. A highly placed official once told me with a chuckle that this had been his view.

> "When I first came out here," he said, "I had a special picture in the back of my mind. You know, a dinner jacket, lots of servants and a big house. It was a real colonial fantasy out of *The King and I*. Of being presented to the king and talking with him about natives and rebellions before we went out to play tennis or shoot tigers."

Similar wish-fulfillment fantasies, nurtured by fairy tales and adventure stories, buzz through the heads of many people overseas.

The Nipa Hut Syndrome

Some people go overseas to help disadvantaged people by working hard under trying super-primitive conditions. (This makes the bringing up of children all the harder, of course.) The concept of a home for these people is a palm-thatched hut in the middle of a jungle. The danger for those who harbor such a fantasy is that they want to be appreciated by the people whom they help. This is a difficult requirement if the host country people believe that the visitors can move easily from their nipa hut to a Hilton Hotel. Changing political conditions that can wipe out the work of a decade in a moment may breed despair. Just such a disheartening result occurred to a group of American doctors in the Middle East; their family medicine network was destroyed by a new minister of health, who felt the need to repudiate all the projects of his predecessor. An especially healthy sense of proportion is needed under such circumstances.

The Gold at the End of the Rainbow Syndrome

Those people who go overseas to make money are, perhaps, the most fortunate Americans, for they have a precise objective. Many of them do amass a considerable amount of money because of high salaries, the low cost of living in many countries, and a favorable income tax break.

The "Eternal Wanderer" Syndrome

Included in this syndrome are the "Flying Dutchman," the "Wandering Jew," and the whirling American or IBM ("I've

Been Moved") types. All are constantly on the go, restless, hoping for something better at the next post. They are on a compulsive search that never ends, one that may give pleasure but seldom gives relief. The bases for their wanderings must be sought for in psychiatric textbooks. Unfortunately, their off-spring often inherit this restlessness.

Although these syndromes are, to some extent, an over-simplification, they may help you define your own motivations more precisely. The following group of questions may further aid the reader in bringing his (or her) reasons for being overseas into better focus.

"How and when did I first get interested in working over-seas?"

"What is most disturbing about going? about not going?"

"What are the advantages and disadvantages for me and my family?"

"What will we carry home from the experience?"

"How will my family be different for having lived overseas?"

If one ponders these questions carefully, answers will emerge to offer needed direction and stability as a family sets off for an overseas career.

It is not possible to judge some motivations healthy and others unhealthy; nor can it be said which lead to success and which foreshadow danger. The basic test is a personal one that combines an assessment of personal ambition and the actual conditions of an overseas post.

But consult your intuition, too. Do you feel a strong pull to live overseas? If the attraction is powerful enough, your choice will have been made, regardless of the seeming realities of a situation, for, as Freud once said, "In the small decisions of life I call upon my judgment; in the large ones I follow the unconscious."

"There are two classes of travel, first class,
or with children."
— Robert Benchley

III

Getting There

BENCHLEY notwithstanding, an entire family can travel in style and comfort. The end-products of a long journey do not necessarily include worn-out parents and cranky children. Nevertheless, a move to a new post differs markedly from a round trip vacation visit to relatives in the United States. Instead of presents for grandma and carefree anticipations, the overseas traveler carries with him concerns about leaving the familiar to confront the unknown. Traveling overseas is best viewed as a serious task. Some reflection on the ideas that follow can make the task of travel, whether for two hours or two months, bearable and even memorable.

Planning

It helps to talk about moving plans with one's entire family, allowing all members a chance to discuss both positive and negative feelings about a move. Each child is entitled to know what will happen well before the departure date. A tried-and-true rule of thumb is to talk with preschoolers about any important change one week before it occurs and with five-to-twelve-year-old children about a month before. Adolescents deserve the full confidence of their parents from the moment any transition is planned.

A three-year-old relates to an overseas move through pictures of camels, llamas, and buildings in a new country. A ten-year-old appreciates the straightforwardness of a father who states openly that a tour overseas means a promotion and a raise in salary. A teenager accepts leaving his friends more gracefully if he knows that his father is seeking a change from a job that has become dull or that his mother yearns for fresh experiences and new friendships. Wise travelers ask their children what they would like to know about the particular country, and library research yields information about the stops en route, which may include exciting visits to Paris or Cairo. Such preliminary "briefing" can be improved by means of a wall map tracing the route you will take. Paste pictures on your walls showing the mountains, buildings, and cities of the new country. Old *National Geographic* magazines—those vicarious travelers' delights—that gather dust in basements become invaluable treasures before a voyage to far-off places. Embassies are pleased to send quanitites of material about their homelands, as are international airlines or foreign tourist offices that operate in the United States.

Many parents encourage their children to read encyclopedia articles and develop projects centered on the country in which they will serve a tour of duty. Involvement is the key to a happy travel experience for parents and children alike. If you can capture the interest of your family, the potential pain of the move will be lessened.

Tears and Sadness

Moving involves separation from familiar people and accustomed surroundings. There is no easy way to escape feelings of loss when a person leaves one home for another. A child's plaintive admission that "ever since you told me about going to Africa, I've worried that I won't have any friends there" can disorganize an entire family. Amid all the hoopla and excitement, a family should be prepared for periods of appetite loss or binges of overeating. Family members may become morose or withdrawn and show their pain by irritability, sleeplessness, fatigue, or just a refusal to go.

A family member in such a state needs sympathetic attention. Perhaps he needs a respite from planning and packing, a time to withdraw into his private space and feel terrible for a while. The trauma may be lessened if someone will listen quietly and say in words or actions, "I'm with you. I know how tough it must be for you right now." Often nothing more is needed and nothing less will do. When feelings are understood and respected, a person can begin to pull out of the doldrums as naturally as the body rids itself of a fever. Experienced parents avoid the twin evils of overtreatment and total disregard. The most effective treatment is simple, accurate recognition of feelings, and tolerance for them.

Fears

Many families put off thinking about a move until the last moment, very much as children procrastinate about doing homework until late at night. Some of this procrastination is related to understandable fears about leaving home. Everyone fears the unknown. But if one can peer for a moment into the unknown and make some sense of its mysteries, the vagaries of travel and moving can be brought into perspective. Fortunately, a definable group of fears seems to be common to most people. Once these are recognized and worked on, travel becomes easy.

Children fret over having to leave *friends*. They become attached to their playmates and cannot conceive of building new friendships. If a child has had difficulty making friends in the past, this concern, though expressed as the sadness of leaving Johnny or Jane, in reality is, "Will anybody like me where I'm going?" A sensitive father or mother can help children articulate these worries.

Children need reassurance that their parents will help them find their way in a new country. Talk with your children about their hopes and fears. Share with them a view that "it's tough to leave friends, and all of us feel sad about that. But I know that we will make new ones in Germany, and we can keep in touch with our old pals while we are away."

In the same sense, it should be remembered that, through a child's eyes, pets are members of a family. Great care should be taken to find a good home for a favorite dog or cat. Children should be told where their animals have gone; secret dispositions of pets may increase a child's anxiety about his own place in his family.

Parents and children alike wonder, "Will I be able to learn the *language?*" The thought of struggling with the pronunciation and vocabulary of a new language can be discouraging, and a large number of American children who have heard only English spoken become anxious when they consider the study of another language. The forceful stresses of French or Italian may embarrass some children, especially those who already have problems with shyness and inhibition. Parents who make a game of language study and participate directly with their children in the learning process have had the greatest success in overcoming this obstacle. The excellent "total immersion" teaching methods now employed further smooth the process. More details about this important subject can be found in chapter 12.

Travel Itself

From the moment a move is decided upon, children deserve as much consideration as adults and as much responsibility as they can handle effectively. Make each youngster responsible for his own luggage and give one sibling the job of counting suitcases. Children want familiar objects around them just as adults do. The usual childhood paraphernalia, such as favorite toys, games, drawing materials, and books, are important. Even boys may enjoy dolls and should be allowed to take along a GI Joe, a cowboy, or a favorite stuffed animal. Girls like to carry special articles of clothing or a travel bag. Many children are comforted by good luck charms in the form of books, pictures, special coins, or jewelry.

Airports and Planes

Airlines, the most convenient and popular method of transportation, regularly assign support personnel to care for sick children and special family needs. Stewardesses and other agents usually are happy to extend themselves for handicapped children or parents who are traveling with the very young.

Airports themselves offer a real fascination to children. The excitement of large gasoline trucks careening around runways, and the takeoffs and landings of immense transatlantic jets hold a child's attention and lessen fear or uncertainty.

Timing

Get to the airport early. Then invoke a conscious laziness once you are there. You can remain reasonably unruffled during the endless and seemingly senseless details of getting bags checked, and waiting in line arranging for passports and health checks, if you prepare a diversion for your family—a riddle book, a number game, or even family meditation.

Getting There

Misunderstandings and bureaucratic tangles multiply in a strange culture. It takes time to make your way through an unfamiliar air terminal, yet many families ignore this fact and come to grief because they arrive late for a departure. Perhaps we Americans make this mistake overseas because we have become too accustomed to our smooth domestic airline schedules, which permit us to crisscross the United Sates in one day. It makes sense to budget one hour more than expected for each international flight. Small children will cry less and an adult's blood pressure will remain at a comfortable level. To improve tempers during long waits, experts counsel adults to bring along puzzles, drawing materials, and other diversions for children and magazines for themselves. The small books on every imaginable subject sold at airport newsstands soothe ruffled nerves when a flight has been canceled and a family must gird itself for a long wait in the hot sun. Some travelers have learned to make up serial stories, with each member adding an episode. Others buy Greek worry beads or movable puzzles to fill tedious delays.

How about the food at smaller airports? One need not depend upon tasteless, non-nutritious, and expensive meals for sustenance. It is possible to carry a supply of powdered milk, crackers, pretzels, juice, cheese, raisins, or other dried fruit. All these can take the place of hot dogs, milk shakes, ice cream, and pie. Later, if the excitement of jet takeoffs has waned, boredom can be lessened by visiting historical and industrial exhibits to be found in many airports.

Flying should be a positive experience that nourishes curiosity and imagination. Parents can promote these qualities in their children with preparation and alertness.

In the Air

Fearful children become tearful children. Toddlers won't cry if they're introduced to a plane after a comfortable time on the ground by parents who express confidence. (Appropriate pre-flight food also helps.) If you compare babies who cry during a flight to those who are quiet, the crying ones usually are a reflection of their parents' discomfort and overprotectiveness. When children, and adults, are prepared for the experience of flying, they will fly with ease.

An overseas journey can be timed so that small children sleep during much of a trip. Show children the toilet, get books for them to read, and tell them when they'll land. The monotony of a long flight can be broken by storytelling or by playing tic-tac-toe or submarine. A pocket tape recorder can be used to store impressions and dialogues or to play pre-recorded material or music for both children and parents. A long flight can offer a pleasing intimacy of experience, a time when families are truly together.

Carry essentials for a trip with you in the cabin of the plane; bags do get misplaced and occasionally lost. Necessary medicines, particularly for children who have allergies or skin disorders, should be kept with you at all times. Many experienced travelers take along a change of shirt and underwear, shaving and washing materials, and food or reading materials that will last for several days in case a plane is delayed or bags get lost.

Who Should Go First?

Should a family travel together? Often a father will precede his family by necessity and use his extra time to find a house and get it in order. What a comfort this can be for a tired, apprehensive mother who arrives with young children after a long plane ride. However, most families choose to fly together in order to share the travel experience; odd events of a family trip become memorable and the thousands of miles of placid, lonely ocean are forgotten.

Getting There

Money Worries

Some travelers become obsessed with the fear of being cheated. Parents who fret over how much to tip communicate their disturbance to their children. Keep your perspective when tipping airport porters; a few extra dollars (even in over-payments) should be budgeted for tips to stewards if a family travels by passenger ship. Some money lost is less important than a child's loss of trust in all host country people because of real or imagined cheating.

Often the traveler may be at fault. On a taxi ride in Washington, D.C., an African diplomat complained that he was taken the long way around to get to his hotel. He berated the cab driver angrily. Only when another passenger explained to him that he was not being charged extra for the necessarily roundabout trip did he calm down.

Take It Easy

Long-time travelers prefer to interrupt a tiring plane trip from America to Africa or Asia with a day in Paris or a weekend in Cairo. Many enjoyable and refreshing recollections will be stored up if one seeks out new experiences and ignores the anxious injunction, "I've got to get there now." If you arrive at a post in a happy frame of mind, with interesting sights and good food under your belt, you will be best able to confront a new country.

Practice

Prepare for a major trip as you would for a rocket launching. Go over details repeatedly. Check on supplies and documents. Plan visits to relatives in the United States as a preparation for moving. Well-prepared children make happy travelers, and, in this mobile time, the ability to travel well is as valuable an accomplishment as a skill in fencing or horseback riding must have been many years ago.

Mainly, pack a positive image of travel along with clothes and books. Don't allow the normal human tendency to resist the change, good or bad, to deter you. Give up the habit of making comparisons; dismiss your uncertainties. Keep in mind the words of the Roman author Petronius, who banished the myriad problems of travel with this counsel:

"Leave thy home O youth, and seek out alien shores!"

"Change doth unknit the
tranquil brow of man."
—Mathew Arnold

IV

The Art of Transition

A WELL-CHARTED arrival at a foreign destination can bring an immediate sense of security, making the transition from the U.S. to another country easy. Such a positive experience doesn't just happen. To illustrate:

On short notice a mother and her three children rushed to join her husband at a new post in Yugoslavia. She recalled the reception this way:

> The children and I tumbled out of the plane in Belgrade in freezing weather after a twenty-hour flight from the United States. We were bushed. But John was at the gate waiting for us, fresh and full of good news. He had a car and obviously knew his way around this strange town. The best part was when he drove us directly to a house, *our* house, that he had made livable, and at the door a beaming maid welcomed us. We promptly sat down to a hot meal served with some of our own silver.

This reassuring scene was the result of thoughtful planning, which smoothes the transition to a new country. Not every problem can be foreseen, of course, and emergencies will inevitably arise later. Gas stoves in Belgrade can spring leaks and the hot water may mysteriously stop flowing.

Life is always an adventure, and we actually remember the tough times we overcame with far greater interest than the easy ones that took no effort. A loss of baggage is transformed into a pleasant encounter by the helpful airline ground agent who provides immediate money to buy a new shirt and tie and commiserates with you about the lost suitcases. A run-down hotel you have been stuffed into by unfeeling employers is transformed into a warm temporary home by a smiling concierge who beguiles your children with magic tricks.

Human beings need reference points when they move: their own home, familiar paintings on the walls, someone they can count on, activities that absorb them, or perhaps a well-prepared hot dinner.

Few family arrivals can be prepared for as well as the one described above, although I suppose all wives hope for such felicitous beginnings. More typically, families will travel together to a foreign destination and enter their new home as a group. In such cases, a husband would be wise to participate in the preparations. His wife is thus not the only family member who assists with the transition. A supportive husband will help with packing, buying children's clothes, or sending out change of address cards. If at all possible, he should guard against the temptation to bury himself in post reports or other overwork during the first few days after arrival.

Here are some of the circumstances that will arise, predictably, in the first few hours and weeks in a new country.

The Welcoming Ceremony and After

If you are lucky, someone from your organization will meet you at the airport, drive you to a hotel, and even provide a first meal. It will make you feel good that your associates care so much about you. However, such special care often dissipates after the first days, and very soon you will be expected to adjust unobtrusively into a schedule of school activities, evening parties, and weekend recreation at an American club or swimming pool. There is even the possibility that heightened anticipations may be marred by the realization that some of the welcomers may not be your kind of people. Disappointments may be in store for the arriving American whose interest in mountain climbing can't be realized in Bangkok or whose skiing passions must be deferred during a tour in Egypt. It makes sense to anticipate the letdown that will surely set in during the first week or month at a new post. It may take time to work through these disappointments and then decide how to use one's time.

Through early involvements with welcoming people, you can acquire important information about schools and doctors, where to buy clothes, how to mail articles, and where children can play or amuse themselves. Many posts publish booklets that describe the stores, play or recreation centers for children, and places for happy family weekend trips. Companies and the U.S. government try very hard to locate houses for their personnel. These dwellings are often ones that have been used previously by individuals in the same organization and come with household help, built-in friends, furniture, and neighborhood activities. The typical American community gives parties to introduce newcomers. Such parties can be a great help, particularly if they include children; then parents won't become separated from their families early in an overseas tour.

Hotels

You may not be lucky enough to have a house available upon your arrival. Instead, you and your family may be booked into a hotel, "only for a few days." Those few days can stretch into weeks or a month and may change a bright welcome into a nightmare, at least for children who find the artificial world of hotel life, with its lack of familiar furniture and absence of play areas, very difficult.

Children left alone often spend their time riding the hotel elevator until they are chased back to their rooms by the hotel manager. The stress may be compounded by a dining room that serves unusual food in a formal and sterile atmosphere. Under such conditions, children become restless, destructive, and irritable. As one woman told me: "Life in a hotel, particularly with preschoolers, is an absolute disaster."

Yet there are solutions even to such difficult situations. Creative families have transformed obligatory hotel living into an adventure. Here is how one mother described her methods:

> After the first days of indulgence and luxury became stale to us, I had the children make their own beds early in the morning. Our two boys were paid by the hotel manager to pick up bottles left in the halls. All of us pitched in to do the washing at a nearby wash-o-mat, and we shared other chores in rotation. We made a rule that we would be out of the hotel by 10:00 each morning to start on language lessons, visits to various parts of the city, and trips to museums. And we evaded the chilly atmosphere of the dining room by having most of our meals sent up to our rooms.

For many travel-wise families, a move to the homelike intimacy of a *pension* can solve these hotel problems. Pension managers generally know a great deal about a city, and they're usually eager to share their knowledge. The majority of families are delighted to exchange the austerity of certain hotels for the home-away-from-home atmosphere of a pension.

A Place to Live You Can Call Home

Although most families fit in wherever their organization drops them, some enterprising souls have always chosen to venture outside the perimeter of their friends or the American community. For them, a critical issue to decide is whether to live in the center of town or in the country.

In a town, one is close to activities and people. By the same token, an American may have to reconcile himself to the fact that he has only a slim chance to develop intimate friendships with host country nationals because much of the world is leery of transient Americans. Also, many large towns are short on play space, and children may be cramped inside houses, often behind walls, during their free time after school.

Almost every city has a "Golden Ghetto" where the so-called rich internationals, mostly Americans, tend to live. This is the path of least resistance and may be the choice of Americans on a short-term assignment or of those whose lives revolve mostly around the international community. The family that attempts to become part of the indigeneous community has a tougher row to hoe. Disappointment may set in unless hopes are modest and resilience considerable.

People who choose to live in the country have greater opportunities to get to know their neighbors. Life in villages is freer, and children tend to meet at play areas or small stores where there is considerable interchange. The hosts may take note that you were interested enough in their nation to move away from living areas chosen by most internationals.

Some people have been disappointed because their hopes were far too high. Here is how one faher expressed it:

> Sure, I wondered what kind of house we were going to live in. Unfortunately, we were misled by my company. If they had said we were going to live in a little two-bedroom house with no air-conditioning, that would be tough but fine. But they led us to think we were going to live in something spectacular, and then we wound up in a little dinky thing. It's pretty discouraging. You say to yourself, "Is this it, is this all?" In our first tour in Peru, we were prepared to live in a cabin. But everyone who had come from Iran told us about the huge houses with big beautiful yards. When we

found that our house wasn't half the size of the one we had in Peru, all of us were sore for months, and we just didn't settle in well.

The First Month

Be aware of the seemingly innocuous but, in fact, critical decisions that must be made when you first arrive at a new post. When you casually agree to an oldest child's request for a bedroom in a distant part of your house, you have separated him from his family; when you slip into a routine of separate mealtimes for children and parents, you have given up an opportunity for family communication. Adults find themselves enmeshed, almost before they know it, in a pattern of obligatory visits to other American families, renewed acquaintances with former friends, and the enticing round of international events and entertainments characteristic of almost any city overseas.

Parents should not permit themselves to fall into passive decision-making. It is wise at first to control each hour of available time. One of the major faults of life overseas is its merry-go-round quality; many familes later want to get off the merry-go-round, but each is afraid to be the first. It is far easier to decline invitations immediately upon arrival than when a family has become part of a group.

Women become the major captives of the social whirl. This is understandable. A husband has his job and children go to school during the day. Meanwhile a wife is often left alone, except for servants who "come with the house." All this may seem like the fulfillment of a dream to women in the United States who are overwhelmed with grocery shopping, dishwashing, and chauffeuring children all day. But the resulting free time can be swallowed up abroad by uncongenial "obligatory" social activities, an endless flow of visitors from the United

The Art of Transition

States who ask identical questions and contrived committee meetings with host country nationals. A wife's surest way to avoid the boredom of such a hectic existence is to take charge of her life when confronting the crisis of transition.

Disappointments Will Occur

Casual encounters may sour a new arrival's view of a foreign country unless he is on guard against making premature judgments. In Mexico, for instance, dubious local characters who watch parked cars may demand exorbitant tips; in southern Italy, a grocer may overcharge an Americano. In Sofia, a taxi driver may make unflattering comments about Americans. Such events will put great demands on an individual's flexibility, loving kindness, and resistance to paranoia.

There will be times when you will think you have been cheated, only to find embarrassingly at a later time that your calculations were in error. Even when you have been overcharged, it is important to keep a sense of perspective. During the first month, it proves useful to give the benefit of the doubt on small money matters to host country people. Some families mentally put aside a certain sum, such as $100, each year in order to cover the petty overcharging and honest errors that will surely occur.

Crises Will Occur

Crises or decision points punctuate normal family life in the United States. The birth of a baby, a change of job, a move— all disturb a family's equilibrium. International life merely highlights the importance of crises because fewer external supports are available. Because the concept of crisis sometimes stirs up thoughts of helplessness and doom, it may be useful to recognize that the word *crisis*, as used in medicine, simply means "turning point." In Greek, the word means "decision" and is free of the ominous connotations we added to it. A turning point may be for the better just as well as for the worse.

If you can accept the occurrence of a crisis as a natural part of life—a time to consider possibilities and make choices—your way will be made infinitely easier. Trouble results only if a person evades or neglects a crisis point when it occurs.

The Ingredients of Successful Transitions

As you read this section, construct a chart for yourself comparing your life in the United States and your anticipation of life overseas. Include all the people and activities that contribute to your feeling of well-being. Then, compare your list with the following one, which was compiled from the combined experience of many people who have lived overseas. Use the differences in the two lists as a starting point in the effort to make a healty transition for you and your family.

The following headings cover most of the supports people need in order to feel comfortable. In moving, many of these supports are lost. The feeling of loss will increase with the distance moved, the finality of a move, and the difficulty of communicating with people in a former home.

SOCIAL ACQUAINTANCES
INTIMATE FRIENDS
COMMUNITY RESOURCES
HELP IN EMERGENCIES
RESPECT FOR COMPETENCE
MEANING IN LIFE
CHANGE

Human beings must grapple continually with the problems of *social isolation*, the need for *close friends*, the search for *useful* resources in a community and *help in emergencies*. We wish to have our *competence* recognized in order to feel that life has *meaning*. Everyone thrives on a measure of diversity and *change*.

Social Isolation

For those who go overseas with a company or the United States government, social isolation is a minor problem. Families are swept up in a flurry of school visits, welcoming activities, social gatherings, and business meetings.

Many people feel far more "American" when they are abroad. Holidays are celebrated with verve and fanfare. U.S. citizens swarm over each other when they meet in order to compare notes on how things are back home. The high visibility of the American community in a foreign country encourages a cohesiveness that amply satisfies the need for social involvement.

Except for families with highly specialized interests—academics, researchers, people who go overseas on their own, or those who do not enjoy the essentially convivial aspects of being an American overseas—there is little need to worry about social isolation. However, for persons who find themselves at loose ends in a new community or feel lost in a large European city, here are possibilities to consider.

—Be sure you have touched all the bases in your adopted community—your children's school, your husband's organization, the host country, and international societies.

—Enroll in a local university or school to study languages, archaeology, history, or music.

—Get involved in tennis, museum-visiting, bridge, or art groups that will bring you in contact with others.

—Contact volunteer agencies likely to need your talents.

Close Friends

Emotional isolation is more difficult to treat than social isolation. "You know you are feeling isolated," one person recalled, "when there are lots of people around but nobody to talk to, nobody you can really open up to."

Most humans need at least one close friend with whom to share complaints about a job or a country. It is helpful to be able to blow off steam about a lovable but sloppy husband or an indecisive boss; it is natural to want to boast about life's triumphs. The key requirement for such an intimate friend or relative is that he be available to listen and not judge.

People don't live together intimately enough overseas to understand the nuances of meaning a person tries to express in a social relationship. Such close knowledge of another person takes a long time to develop and includes a lot of "soul" understanding that can't really be put into words. Overseas life is a kind of showcase existence in which people are always on their "best" behavior; in fact, this may not be their best behavior, but only their most stilted. Intimacy is therefore a rare quality to find under such conditions.

One executive put it this way:

Here in Asia we all watch each other too closely. Call it a fishbowl syndrome. People won't admit they have problems with drinking or with their children because they feel their jobs are on the line. Most people want to hide their problems, and in a way they are right. There is just no place to talk about the things that bother you, much less the little things that make you feel good. You always have the sense that somebody is going to judge you, somebody that doesn't know you very well. People just want to get through the year or through their tour and get themselves out. It's a feeling that they just don't want anyone else to know what their problems are.

Husbands and wives might seem to be natural candidates for intimacy, but often life doesn't work out that way. Many couples just don't know each other well. Dr. Eric Berne, author of

The Art of Transition

Games People Play, once estimated that, for most couples, fifteen minutes of intimacy in a lifetime together seems a fairly good record. A careful study of the habits of normal American families concluded that the average unit—husband, wife, and two children—spent only twenty-six minutes each week in intimate conversation, whereas they consumed hours in scheduling activities, fixing screen doors, and taking shirts to the laundry. It is the profound need for intimate discussion, someone to talk with openly about life, that has made psychotherapy so important in our contemporary world, for, in psychotherapy, the therapist asks a patient to "tell me about yourself," and then really listens.

Some special American intimacy patterns do not thrive well in all foreign soils. In certain respects, we ask for more personal and private information than most other people in the world. We inquire about some topics—money, sex, or possessions, for example—that Latin Americans or Europeans rarely discuss in open conversation with new acquaintances. A seasoned overseas businessman in Rome shed a piercing light on this difference between Americans and other nationals. Here is how the executive expressed it:

> I think it's definitely an American personality trait to try to establish communication by divulging intimacies, and I think it's more a reflection of our lack of larger interests. That is, we resort to small talk and gossip because we don't know how to speak about other things. For example, I was having dinner with a couple recently, a businessman and his wife. We talked about this and that but nothing much got going until his wife excused herself for a few minutes and then the husband went into great detail about the difficulty she had in getting pregnant for the second time. As I understood it, he was trying to pull me into a kind of closeness, a comradeship with him, but then he waited for me to reciprocate and say something, I suppose, about how much I disliked my company or about my dandruff or an ingrown toenail.

Obviously, if you find yourself engrossed by the politics or art of a country, you may not long for the intimacy just described. How can the craving for greater closeness be satisfied? To begin with, husbands and wives first might look to themselves to analyze if each might be able to satisfy the other's needs. If a couple lacks intimacy, perhaps a problem needs to be resolved before leaving on an overseas tour. If closeness is impossible, each spouse must look for other means to ease the tensions that inevitably accumulate abroad. In some instances, married couples make great strides by sharing new activities that stimulate them both. Hiking or shared hobbies can often lead to a better contact, even for couples who have lived together for years. Similarly, danger brings two people together.

Since relatives, particularly parents and siblings, are our first intimates, keep them in mind when you feel the need for a little gossip. Keep a journal to share with them. Use audiotape cassettes as a way to communicate some of your stream-of-consciousness thoughts. Implore relatives to respond in kind so that you can have a two-way conversation.

For others, it proves worthwhile to cultivate at least one friend in the community with whom to share an interest, such as pottery or reading, and arrange to see that friend at a regular time.

Resources in the Community

You need to find someone who can direct you to a good hardware store, a well-stocked record shop, a place to buy furniture. You may not know where to look for painting materials, kitchen utensils, or the kind of food your family enjoys. It can be annoying if you don't know how to reach into a community to find these referral agents and perplexing if you haven't even recognized the problem. Indeed, many people experience a kind of environmental isolation without being aware of what is missing.

Many U.S. communities abroad actually provide lists of

useful shops and services. If such information is not yet available, it may pay to develop the list yourself in cooperation with other families. Many knowledgeable expatriates utilize trips out of the country to obtain equipment they need. Families in Asia consider Hong Kong a warehouse from which they buy their stereo components and binoculars. American families in Europe gather up trunkloads of books on their visits to London. It also makes good sense to obtain addresses of mail order suppliers of needed articles *before* leaving the United States.

Help in Emergencies

One bad experience with acute illness or an accident at the start of an overseas tour can sour a family forever on a country. A wise embassy official told me, "If someone in a family gets sick on arrival or they have a bad experience with the local police at the start, then they kind of withdraw into themselves and they just will not go out again. I've seen it happen many times."

The embassy official advises to secure the name of a pediatrician or physician, as well as American insurance agents and reliable garages, *before* the emergency arises. Such names and addresses are available from American embassies, consulates, chambers of commerce, and other U.S. outposts. An American may need to be able to borrow money at once if there is an acute problem. During the absence of a spouse, panic may result. Yet, even such emergencies can be prepared for. The names of American banks are readily available. In this respect, travelers should check on insurance before leaving the United States. Keep a bank account open and plan for any emergency drafts of money you might possibly require. Be sure that all legal documents are in order and available to you. Likewise, you can find out about the medical care in the country to which you are going from an employer. Check with your family doctor at home to be sure that medical documents will be available if needed. Some Americans actually go one medical step further. Here is good advice from a seasoned international person: "The best thing I ever did was to take a first aid course. I now know how to take care of minor problems in my children and no longer panic over rashes and fevers." (See Chapter 13 for further details on medical needs.)

A Feeling of Competence

We all need a continuing affirmation that what we think and do are worthwhile. If we don't think that our competence is recognized, we will feel little self-worth. If your strong point is gardening, it becomes important to find a plot of land to till and others who share your green thumb; if it is woodworking, a workbench and the search for other cabinetmakers prove helpful.

People with special interests may feel isolated in some overseas situations. The typical overseas person today, in contrast to the consuls during the time of Stendhal or Hawthorne, calls upon skills that are primarily social in nature. The abilities to make small talk, to be pleasing, and to cope with repetitive social functions head the list of desirable accomplishments. Few people overseas are particularly interested in discussing books or poetry at greath length. The skills of a Chaucer expert may be of little use in Ethiopia. A bassoon player may feel isolated in Pakistan.

The feeling of competence may be enhanced by defining serious personal interests and pursuing these interests. Anyone can eventually discover kindred spirits anywhere in the world, although it may take dogged effort.*

Americans can always attempt to make their special skills

---

* Even a bassoon player can now find some company through the Overseas Directory published by Amateur Chamber Music Players, Inc., P.O. Box 547, Vienna, Virginia 22180.

known in a community. A woman may wish to organize a flower show or a needlepoint display, or to visit the local hospital and convince the administrator that he needs a social worker. To stick to other particular interests and pursuits requires pure persistence.

Meaning

Humans are thinking beings for better or worse. Our lives must have a sense of direction and meaning or we fall prey to anxiety. We need to feel that our work is worthwhile and has some continuity.

In times of danger and uncertainty—a period of revolutionary activity or anti-American outbreaks—the panic that may sweep a community stems from a loss of meaning. A change of government may wipe out a decade of humanitarian striving and, in the process, destroy one's sense of accomplishment. Similarly, political difficulties in the United States can be disheartening. As one foreign service officer put it: "You will meet a lot of disappointed idealists overseas, people who find things going on in Washington hard to swallow and wish they represented a better society."

Psychiatrists agree that people need goals, both immediate and long-term. It thus makes sense to prepare a list of goals, a kind of personal or family "five-year plan," and then attempt to achieve those objectives. A tour of duty should be seen as a whole. This requires a realistic inventory of what one hopes to accomplish. Goal achievement can be further improved by establishing a progression to one's days and plans. Short-term goals come first. Also, use a long-term calendar to keep yourself focused on the direction of your life. In dark times, recall the audacity and optimism you showed by deciding to live overseas.

The Need for Change

We all require continuing challenges in our lives in order to maintain a dynamic sense of perspective about ourselves. People perk up when they find new friends or set out on a changed career direction. The monotony of a rigid, totally predictable life, no matter how important it may be, can be devastating. The person who does exactly the same thing each day is a candidate for boredom and for being boring to others. Such an individual may also become a candidate for depression. The need for the new can often be satisfied in simple ways that are available to anyone with enough curiosity in his environment. Some Americans' solution is to ferret out new learning experiences; they look into a country's often fascinating crafts: learning to weave, dye clothes, make pottery, and so on. Or they're alert enough to seek out local clubs or groups that encourage new members to share a sports activity (such as soccer in Latin America) or to acquire skills in new regional dances (such as certain dances in Africa or in many of the Iron Curtain countries).

One expatriate points out that sometimes the *children's* ideas are fresher than those of an adult. He says, "Solicit activity suggestions from every member of the family!"

Fortunately, overseas life offers extensive novelty and adventure so that, in most cases, the situation is the opposite one, creating an overload of new experiences. The newcomer abroad simply does not have the time to assimilate experiences and make them his own. Many families learn only smatterings of a language, partially explore archaeological sights, make one quick foray into the museums, and then stop because of a newer, competing interest. If your family is battered by too many stimuli, schedule periods to do nothing more than stay home together and regroup on a weekend. There is no need to overload your family with disconnected activities that eat up time and leave no happy residue.

In short, the transition from one culture to another requires work and a real willingness to adapt oneself to new conditions. It means that one must accept change and encourage similar acceptance in all members of a family.

This chapter has stressed the general principles of transition. The next will focus on the nuts and bolts of settling in.

"And should I then presume? And how
should I begin?"
     —T. S. Eliot

Finding Your Way in a New Country

WE AMERICANS are often welcomed overseas because we represent a unique style in speech, movement, and dress. We are different and there is no need to hide our individuality. "Be yourself" is a good maxim, but knowledge of the ways of another country will help you understand its people better and ease your daily contacts with them.

The important characteristics of culture are taken for granted by natives and are learned only painfully, if at all, by most visitors. You may or may not choose to become involved in the ways of a country, but it is perilous to ignore them. Therefore, let us look at some points that almost belong to an etiquette book, except that we will examine custom rather than costume, children rather than the placing of knives and spoons.

Children

International children tend to be quieter and "better be-
haved" than youngsters in the United States. Adults expect
children to shake hands, stand up when spoken to, and remain
quiet at other times. There is a much greater emphasis on formality than is typical of most regions of the United States.
Some parents help their children adapt to changed expectations by teaching a crash course in party manners for use when
needed.

Despite the formality expected of youth, some adults may
startle you by their intrusive relationships with children. El-
derly grandmothers in Moscow think nothing of striding up to
a baby in a stroller and fussing over its clothes without asking
permission from the infant's mother. In many countries,
adults feel free to criticize the behavior of a child anywhere
and anytime.

Clothes

There was a time when the button-down shirt and miniskirt
were trademarks of Americans abroad; such fashions set us
apart from other international travelers. Mothers had to decide
whether to bring American-style clothes for their offspring or
to appear less conspicuous by adopting host country or European fashions. At the same time, we have exported blue jeans
and moccasins so effectively that it is difficult to tell an American youngster from any other throughout the world. The job
of buying clothes for an overseas tour has been made easier
because the United States has captured the world, at least in
children's wear; though, according to many observers, American youth are still the most conformist and the quickest to
adopt fads. In any international school overseas, the host

country nationals stand out because they seem to be dressed with more care and individuality than Americans.

During the settling-in period, parents will have to learn new clothing and shoe sizes. Overweight or extra tall teenagers will despair when they can't find clothes ample enough to fit their big frames. Certain styles—striped tennis shoes or imprinted T-shirts—will be unobtainable.

The Spoken Language and the Real Language

Americans often speak louder than other nationals, except perhaps the Germans. When we are not understood, we show the unfortunate trait of raising our voices in the mistaken hope that decibels will ring other bells in the minds of our hearers. To be sure, we sometimes assume shouting will somehow make English intelligible to a person who does not understand English.

Whole books have been written about what we communicate by gesture, tone of voice, and body movements.* As you settle into a new community, pay particular attention to *how* you relate, not simply to what you say. The rewards of such attention in accurate, acceptable communication can be immense.

Street Relationships

A blonde American child's hair will be admired and caressed innumerable times in a country of dark-haired youngsters, particularly if the blonde hair is long. People will touch and hold your clothing in order to feel the difference in texture and think nothing of asking how much your suit cost.

In the same vein, American teenage girls must learn to tol-

* E. T. Hall, *The Silent Language* (New York: Doubleday, 1959); A. G. Smith, ed., *Communication and Culture* (New York: Holt, Rinehart and Winston, 1966).

erate the noisy attention of young Italian men who mean no harm. The daughter of an American commercial attaché in Rome learned how to avoid the occasional (and locally accepted) pinch; she would simply avoid large crowds and packed buses. As for the gauntlet of young Italian males, she'd just walk faster or avoid the confrontations.

Children will encounter a different situation in the streets of certain Caribbean nations. Here, young Americans must learn to ignore the angry, racially motivated stares. How about certain developing countries in Asia or Africa? Unless Americans happen to be caught up in a local revolution or anti-American disturbance, the chance of facing violence will be extremely slight. Even the possibility that natives may throw stones at American youngsters seems slim. All the same, it is important to teach children how to deal with such an occurrence. As one parent said, "I just told them to run away, and reminded them that the same kinds of things happen in the United States."

Many an American girl has heard foul epithets spoken to her in Urdu or Farsi and been poked in ways that can only be approximated by the intensity of the jostling that occurs in New York subways.

Some young Americans actually invite difficulties by walking on the wrong street or wearing inappropriate clothes. A short skirt, for example, is inappropriate in a Muslim country.

In order to keep some perspective, remember that the first assembly in many New York private schools is devoted to a discussion of how to give up your wallet to a potential mugger and then get away as fast as possible with no complaints.

Class and Social Distinctions

Many countries, and American communities in those countries, are far more class- or, perhaps, hierarchy-conscious than we are in the United States. Though the children of tractor drivers, company vice-presidents, and ambassadors will go to school together and be close friends, host country children whose families occupy a higher or lower socioeconomic status than visiting Americans may present problems in relationships. Families must learn who can and who can't be included as social companions for their children. And, despite our democracy, the pecking order in a post becomes quite important because of the closed-in quality of the whole society. Families who choose host country nationals as their primary friends may find themselves misunderstood by the other Americans at a post. There are no easy solutions to these concerns, but attention to them may soothe bruised feelings and promote understanding.

When people expect more from a society than it can give, complaints arise such as this one told to me by an irate American businessman: "Damn it," he said, "I don't have any local friends. We are never invited to an Afghan's house. I see Afghans at work and sometimes for lunch in a bazaar, but I've never seen their houses; I don't know what their wives look like or even know their children."

Awareness should be the watchword so that you are not offended by host country mores and don't expect more from your hosts than they can offer.

How To Get To Know a Country

The history, politics, and geography of a country would not seem to be particularly mainstream psychological issues, but knowledge of the place where you live will help your understanding of the people and their customs and avert irritation and unhappiness.

Each family has a characteristic way of approaching new experiences. Some families spend an inordinate amount of time preparing for a post and run the risk of becoming jaded before they reach a new country. Others jump in without any knowledge and are at the mercy of bewildering newness and complexity. Some families never define their interests abroad and flounder during their entire time overseas.

One of the most useful techniques for getting to know a country is to make an inventory of the pastimes your family engages in regularly in the United States. What sports do you play? What do you do with your time, not only during the week but on weekends? How do your children use the facilities of their home town? Are they involved with museums, music lessons, television, art galleries? After you have made such an inventory, inquire about similar activities available in your adopted country. Make contact with groups involved in leisure activities that your family enjoys and look for ways to fill the voids when you can't practice the hobbies and other interests you pursued in the United States.

If you move to Kenya from a crowded city in the United States, sell your ice skates and learn something about hiking, camping, animals, or fishing before you do. If you settle in Iran, store your scuba diving gear and, instead, study archaeology or carpet-weaving techniques. Dig into the activities of the local people and learn about their characteristic interests.

Exploring a New Country

Where do people get together in your new town or region? Is it the town square, a block of coffee houses, a theater district, an athletic field? Stroll around and become an expert in mini-geography.

How does politics affect the lives of local people? Will you be free to discuss your political views? Just as some Americans still find it difficult to move from North to South in the United States because of political disagreements, a move overseas will surely stir up areas of conflict. Fortunately, in some countries—England and France, for example—political discussions are part of the way of life, and many Americans develop a keen interest in government because of the availability of such discussions.

Learn something about the major artistic concerns in your adopted country. An interest in national customs, holidays, dances, or eating habits will familiarize you with a new country, and your knowledge of local folkways will endear you to the host country people.

Americans, it is said, tend to gloss over world history, except as it affects the United States. Moving to a foreign country gives one a fine opportunity to change that attitude held by others and, in the process, make one's work and life more stimulating. The history of a country, particularly its social history, will afford sensitive insights into the people abroad. Where do they come from? What are they like? What political and military figures have made them what they are? Young children enjoy learning about emperors, wars, and explorations. If given the chance, they will spend endless time exploring fortifications.

Consult the Department of State, the United States Information Agency, and other government agencies that can tell you about crops, economics, fisheries, international trade, and native handicraft in the area where you will live. Learn about the characteristic sports of a country and the terrain and rainfall you might expect.

Pick a specific topic or field of interest in the country where you will live and become expert in that area. If you want to learn about the art of Germany, be sure that you gain a good grasp of the art of a particular period that interests you. Is it painting of the fifteenth century? Is it baroque churches? If so, will the children become interested in baroque churches or Renaissance altarpieces? Young people often become fascinated with architecture when the religious shrines, palaces, and forts in a town can be related to particular wars, revolutions, and invasions.

Seek out people who share your enthusiasms. Attend museum lectures or experimental film showings; visit the haunts of music lovers or gun collectors. Persistence will bring congenial companions who will welcome your interest in sharing their activities.

Even if you have been slow to utilize the resources in a country, it is never too late to start. It is possible to write someone in the United States to obtain more data and background. Consult a state travel agency, government bureau, or library for details. In many nations, it is also possible to make friends with the local people; Denmark (to name one of many examples) officially organizes a "meet the Danes" program, which allows visitors to mingle with their professional counterparts in Denmark. For an American who speaks a foreign language, other friendship avenues exist in associations and fraternal clubs such as the Lion's, Rotary, and Kiwanis.

All of these thoughts were epitomized in a plea made to me by a young American who had lived overseas all of his life. He said, "Tell Americans to immerse themselves in a culture, to learn about the language, dance, archaeology, art, and music in the place where they will live. Then they will feel comfortable. Otherwise, they will turn on the American community for all of their satisfactions and probably be dissatisfied in the end."

The Troubles

What can happen when you don't get settled well? "I suddenly lost all perspective," said a young woman who had trouble finding her way in a new environment, even though she had lived abroad much of her life. She continued, "It was a pretty hard blow because I had never been knocked down in my life before. Everything friends would tell me would make me really homesick. I had no concept of the dirt and filth, of people urinating in the street, or of the way they treat animals here. The food was terrible and they didn't repair the toilet I had to use for three months."

An overseas physician ruefully recalled a painful family situation. He said: "I remember this very handsome, outgoing couple, who just began to come unglued and they showed it in their demandingness. They insisted on this school, that house. Nothing was quite right for them. When their house wasn't perfectly spotless, they demanded that someone come in and clean it up immediately. Whenever any of their children got sick, they expected me to be over there for the first cough. I knew they wouldn't make it. And they didn't. Not because of their house or sickness, but because they weren't prepared and weren't willing to bend a little."

A range of feelings surfaces in the course of an overseas stay. Bewilderment may be followed by anger, curiosity by ardent involvements, devotion by disenchantment. Many reactions are so predictable in time and intensity that a series of changes or nodal points can be outlined for typical overseas situations. For example, psychiatrists who consulted with the Peace Corps noted that volunteers went through a characteristic cycle of reactions to their posts. First came a crisis of engagement during the initial months of overseas service; then, after about six months, came a crisis of total involvement, at which time the volunteer tended to turn away from American supports and interests; and, finally, a crisis of disengagement occurred at about one and a half years, when it was necessary to make preparations to leave. Such periods of crisis or uncertainty normally accompany the necessity for change, and an understanding of them can make a transition more satisfactory.

Finding Your Way in a New Country

Exciting Differences, Shocking Differences, Intriguing Differences

One family may be so swept up in a country's attractions that they never evaluate what is happening to them. Another newly arrived family may so immerse itself in the American community that nothing of the country itself—its people and uniqueness—are appreciated. Members of such a family often reach the end of a tour feeling cheated and deprived because they learned nothing of the country in which they lived.

The entrance into a new culture may be reminiscent of those common anxiety dreams in which a person finds himself walking naked through a crowded street. Many people experience this feeling of nakedness and perplexity, and undergo a period of ineffectiveness when they come to a situation that is novel to them. The difference between expectation of what a new life will offer and its actuality can be difficult.

Certain intriguing aspects of a country can bring up wishes that are difficult to satisfy. One man remembered his introduction to Asia this way: "The naked children were very much of an attraction; no not an attraction, I mean strange. The people didn't wear many clothes, but I wondered what was underneath the single garment women wore. I really wanted to pick one up, but I never did."

Even when language itself offers no barriers, our topics of conversation may challenge the ingenuity of host country friends. Listen to some Americans as they travel overseas and comment on life. One person converses entirely through the use of questions: "What is a good restaurant in Warsaw? How do you get things wholesale here?" Another will specialize in disparaging remarks: "John never is on time." A third will speak of his family incessantly: "My uncle married his third wife and then started his hardware business; it wasn't started

55

after his second wife." Yet another person talks of nothing but his experiences in the "war," oblivious to whether it was the First World War, Second World War, Korean, or Civil War. Finally, there is a pattern that is almost normal for overseas Americans: that of making comparisons between a present place and one previously visited: "I wonder what people in SriLanka who make fifty dollars a year would think if they could see the yachts in this harbor?" or, "This view isn't as good as the one of Manila Bay." Such conversational themes make it hard going in some countries. Perhaps we should offer our host country counterparts courses in understanding Americans.

By reaching out in a culture, we can discover and savor the recurrent topics of interest so that we can explore new ideas under the lead of our hosts and not place them under the pressure of responding to our preoccupations. After all, one of the prime reasons for traveling is to learn to think in new categories and explore fresh possibilities.

". . . termination of participation of Americans in any particular binational (overseas) situation is more highly correlated with unsatisfactory family adjustments than with unsatisfactory work relationships."
—Drs. Ruth and John Useem

Family Adjustments

A MOVE OVERSEAS may exact a heavy toll of suffering unless all members of a family work at making their adjustment a successful one. Unfortunately, many people deal with family stresses by refusing to acknowledge them. Attention to the personal problems inherent in uprooting the family is often neglected as family members become overwhelmed with physical preparations. Fathers, particularly, may mistakenly conclude that they can move an entire family thousands of miles without any fuss because they have become accustomed to flying in a single day from one end of a country to another to transact business. But family business is a time-consuming affair in which it is difficult to close deals quickly.

Because intra-family relationships are so important, they deserve special consideration in overall planning. It is an evasion for family members to say they cannot afford to spend time on the management of their relationships with one another because they must master new jobs, a new language, and a new culture.

Family Life in the United States

In order to understand family needs overseas, we must first consider family relationships in the United States. A typical family might include a mother, father, children, a dog who barks at night, grandparents who look forward to regular visits of their grandchildren, possibly alcoholic uncles, someone in need of financial or emotional help, and various other sick, old, or divorcing relatives and their children. A businessman in the United States may be absent all day while he works at an abstract job in a large, glass-sheathed building. When he returns home at night, he may help with some household chores, play with his children, or take his wife out to the movies. On weekends he may play golf, mow the lawn, paint furniture, watch television, or choose other private activities in which his family can share. He is responsible only to himself and his family.

Mothers keep more than busy as they drive children to school, get the refrigerator repaired, arrange for music lessons and friends for their offspring, and pursue their own interests. With what time is left, Father and Mother can begin to concentrate on those great issues that truly define happy families—intimacy, affection, genuineness, and appreciation of the individuality of all the family members.

Children spend many hours in school, depending upon their age, and much of the rest of their time out in the community. They prowl around local stores and learn a great deal about life from the culture of shopping centers and advertising media.

Relatives are important in the United States, more important than we often recognize. They are sources of assistance when a child is born or sickness hits. They reassure family members that they are not isolated and can give the kind of unquestioning support that is crucial at certain times in life. Christmas, Thanksgiving, birthdays, and graduations are often defined by the presence of grandmothers, cousins, and other family members. This large family unit suffers total disruption with a move overseas, where many of these supports are no longer available.

A *Family Overseas*

In the transition to an overseas life, a father typically immerses himself further in a career that broadens to include, in addition to his primary job, the matters of language, international economics, the bureaucracy of a new country, and his role as a visible representative of the United States. Overwhelmed with charts, books, language records, and new hopes, a father may not find himself easily diverted to the problems of an eight-year-old daughter about to lose her best friend, a wife who must give up an interesting part-time job, or a son who can no longer hope to play high-school football.

Some comments made to me by children overseas highlight this view:

My father works extremely hard and very long hours, so I never have known him very well. We never share any real family activity with him.

I don't have a recollection of my father when we lived in Europe and Asia. I never remember seeing him in any of those places. He doesn't fit in at all. My mother was around a good deal, and I divided my time between her and the maid.

Throughout my early life, I never recalled my father's being with us. When we were in the United States we played baseball together, but in those foreign countries there was never much that he did with us that I can remember. My mother is the person I talked to and she was the one I took my problems to.

These are fairly strong indictments; unfortunately, they are echoed and re-echoed by overseas children and their mothers.

Fathers may become inordinately busy and lose contact with their families. The key to maintaining imtimacy is the father's willingness to involve himself with his wife and children and to spend significant time with them. His ability to relate to his whole family depends, of course, upon the amount of closeness he and his wife shared before their move and how much they can accommodate to each other as they settle in overseas.

Happily, many families recount a positive story of their overseas experience. One mother told me:

> We had a marvelous time. My husband was ever so busy, yet we went on family picnics or long hikes on weekends. Saturday and Sunday were practically inviolate. Maybe he had to go down to the office to check cables or something, but we would be waiting and get started when he got home. My husband insisted that nothing was to be scheduled for Saturday or Sunday outside of the family, because that time belonged to all of us. There is just no substitute for that chance to be together.

If an American mother's job seems to combine that of a bus driver, chambermaid, nursemaid, and counselor, the opportunity to live overseas may appear to be a fairy tale come true, with a woman in the role of a princess whose life moves each day from tennis court and swimming pool to bridge table and cocktail parties. Indeed, women overseas often find that they can fulfill social, artistic, creative, or indolent dreams. But because of the availability of household help in many countries, even previously devoted mothers may neglect the primary needs of their families and discover some nightmarish qualities in their dreams.

Children adjust most easily as they move from their major task in the United States, which is schooling, to exactly the same task at an overseas post. They leap enthusiastically into new experiences, and their natural curiosity helps them to make quick and happy transitions to a new society in the first few months.

Relatives left behind may complicate a move. Sick grandparents, alcoholic uncles, and shared property arrangements are no longer direct concerns for the overseas family. A family overseas sheds painful burdens but also loses a sense of participation in decisions affecting relatives.

Men and women who move abroad separate from their parents a second time. Those who recall the often wrenching experience of leaving home to get married will also recognize how disturbing it may be to once again relinquish a closeness with parents. This relinquishment, particularly when it occurs without any realistic hopes of immediate reunions, may result in loneliness and guilt.

Previously submerged ambitions and marital problems may surface when a family makes a move, just as ants crawl out when you overturn a stone. Couples who go overseas with the thought that "we'll give it one last chance before we quit" may find that they have added to their woes rather than resolved them, for a long-distance move adds rather than relieves stress in a marriage. By heading for the far corners of the earth, a person doesn't jettison his problems but takes them along.

Husbands and wives frequently find that their paths diverge when they step onto foreign soil. Both may become absorbed in the effort to understand a new culture and gain some place in a society that feels no responsibility or commitment to accept them. This absorption is to the detriment of their involvement with each other and with their children. A man may channel all of his energy into his career and the reawakened challenge of great external achievement, particularly when he becomes "the agricultural representative of the United States of America" instead of just a teacher of botany in Maryland. Many men thrive on the fulfillment of long-dormant wishes for power and leadership, and, in the process, neglect their wives and children.

When women feel superfluous to their households, yet have

little opportunity to pursue careers, their fantasies may turn toward romantic fulfillments. If they discover that their husbands are bewitched by power, wives may search in other directions to be charmed. Mature and prudent spouses examine their individual positions overseas and decide to look to each other and to their children for the affection and shared interests that define a happy marriage.

Overseas people need to seek security in their own identities and relationships in order to withstand the new stresses on their lives. Freud once said that six people sleep in every marital bed, by which he meant that the parents of a newly married couple were symbolically present in a marriage. In an overseas situation, that bed must sleep even more people—perhaps the ambassador, the head of the company a man works for, or the woman who dominates the community, for all these important people regulate a family's lifestyle to a far greater extent than they would in the more private and informal life of the United States.

A single, pivotal factor makes the greatest difference between a well-adjusted family in the United States and an unhappy or psychologically disturbed one overseas. This factor is the change in family organization that places a child overseas in the orbit of a housekeeper and potentially deprives his mother of a functional role in the life of her family and household. As adults become busy in a new country, they find it only too convenient to delegate the caretaking of children to others. Experienced and confident caretakers who seem to know exactly what to do often intimidate Americans, for Americans are uncomfortable about giving orders to other adults. Family members may find themselves enslaved to the needs, whims, and practices of their hired help; and eventually learn that to buy out of that slavery is extremely costly to the lives of everyone. Chapter 8, "Another Mother," covers these concerns in detail.

Family Adjustments

This may seem like a bewildering catalog of problems to juggle when you would prefer to leaf through issues of *National Geographic*, but attention paid to these issues—and many of them are resolved easily and naturally by a cohesive family—can smoothe the way for a happy overseas tour. An overseas businessman once told me an excellent prescription his family employed to confront the disruption they faced regularly. He said:

> In the situation of continuous change that our overseas corporation subjects my family to, most of the priorities are also subject to change, and each person in my family is called upon truly to be in touch with himself in order to know which priorities are absolutely steadfast, and which can be modified.

Remedies to such disruption can be sought prior to the departure from the U.S. One major countermeasure is awareness of the forthcoming changes within a family. It is possible, for instance, to chart for the family as a group some of the possible changes, which may bring about new personal relationships as well. Priorities should be established, too. And a family must be aware of the different issues that influence their happiness overseas. All this can be done in writing on the chart.

Here are some components:

Care of Children

Parents who hope to travel independently of their children when overseas may find themselves in conflict between their own desires and the legitimate needs of their young. A mother may hop to Paris on weekend trips without her preschooler, and then feel guilty about leaving him with the baby-sitter. Teenagers and other young adults fare better than infants or small children during month- (or months-) long absences of their elders. After all, affluent American parents can place

63

older children in excellent private schools, particularly in Europe. The boarding schools (known as *internate*) of Switzerland, for instance, are stimulating enough to work out splendidly for intelligent, mature American high-school-age youngsters, permitting Mother and Father to be absent for several summer months. If the relationship between these children and their parents is a strong, secure, loving one, little damage will be done during limited periods of separation. Youngsters with divorced parents, or chronically neglected children, present a somewhat different situation. The adult's absence for a whole summer may accentuate already present emotional problems. A *few days* of parent absenteeism can hardly hurt children from ages three to eight, unless the trip is made to seem an escape from the child or disapproval of the child is voiced before parting. One-to-three-month-long stays at impersonal nurseries or *kinderheime* (children's hotels) may have some damaging effects. If the child feels "dumped," and isn't contacted by his parents for weeks, insecurity will rear its head, lingering for years and often for life. Many lonely adults, especially in Europe, can trace the feeling of being unloved to such early traumas.

Relatives

Once they are four thousand miles from Indianapolis, even the best-treated American children in Iran will at first miss not only their friends at home but perhaps certain relatives as well. Some preschoolers I interviewed in far-flung countries told me that they missed "Grandma's presents." They also longed for Grandpa's affection, which cannot be substituted by correspondence. The children's own fathers and mothers may have to face other gaps in their new lives.

Some young couples still lean strongly on their parents for advice and support. Once out of the U.S., these couples must be able to cope alone with the myriad problems found in developing countries. A mother must adapt to new formulas and bottles for her baby and learn to shop according to the local economy, which can be tricky indeed in certain areas. For instance, a twenty-three-year-old father who at home would still seek counsel from his own father regarding tools and repairs will now have to get along on his own. The separation from stateside in-laws can be beneficial if the relatives themselves constituted problems at home. A tour of overseas duty can shed a new and often healing light on such relationships.

Values

"I'm afraid that being away from the United States for so long a time will make a real snot out of my son," said one mother. "He thinks he's hot stuff already because he's traveled extensively and learned to speak three languages." Such opinions are not universal, but a great deal of travel can occasionally bring on an air of superiority. A parent must guard against it. However, it can be safely said that the children of overseas Americans are often more sophisticated than stateside youngsters.

Career

Women who give up career and educational possibilities to move overseas need husbands who are willing to participate in a restructuring of the marital relationship that will give each member an opportunity to find the satisfactions he or she needs.

Here is an example of how the chart might look with some of the issues it might include:

Family Change Inventory

	United States	Overseas
Work	Variable	Increases
Ambition	Variable	Increases
Time Away from Home	Variable	Increases
Control of Free Time	Total	Needs Constant Attention
Representational Role	Absent	Present
Intimacy	Variable	May Decrease
Relatives	Present	Absent
Friends	Present	Absent
Servants	Absent	Often Present
A Mother's Career	Homemaker ±	Greater Discretionary Time
Supervision of Children	Mother	Servants
Jobs for Mothers and Teenage Children	Present	Absent

Together with a pinpointing of changes in family relationships and needs, one must pay attention to this series of usual nodal points that define the course of an overseas career. Here are some questions that often arise and that require individual answers.

Leaving for Overseas

What family problems will you leave behind you? Can you help an aged mother in a nursing home by remaining at home, or is it necessary to give precedence to the priorities of your own development? Can you keep in touch with doting grandparents through regularly planned visits both ways or tape recordings of grandchildren sent at intervals? Is it important for you to own a house in the United States, or do you feel comfortable about burning your bridges to your home town?

Settling In

The wife of a highly mobile overseas husinessman gave this advice:

> When you first get to a post, there is a tendency to get out and move in the community. But I've always turned the tables and entertained at home the first six weeks. Then you don't have to leave a screaming, hysterical child in the hands of a housekeeper she doesn't know. And, since your things haven't arrived from your last post, you can get away with murder by entertaining simply. When I had small children, we attended only the events we absolutely could not avoid.

Many families continue this pattern. A father told me:

> My wife and I are not great ones to go out unless it's something we have to do. We entertain a lot at home, and the kids have always helped to plan the parties. We make up for the fact that relatives are not around at Thanksgiving or Christmas by having whole families, young and old, join in with us. I think we're a closer family because we read together, do things together, and don't depend on outside things like television to entertain us.

When husbands dive into their work, children disappear into school, and the household organization is taken over by servants who know the native language (and, therefore, do the buying in the markets and negotiate with handymen who paint the rooms and fix the electrical appliances), women may feel that they are left high and dry. "Women are the ones who suffer," said a woman with substantial overseas experience. "They feel so useless when they get overseas, and then they turn to drinking or they become depressed. Some turn to promiscuity and get into complicated relationships that seem always to end in guilt and trouble."

A woman who had observed such patterns offered these observations and suggestions:

> When you first move overseas, or make any move, you no longer
> have your friends, your relatives, your activities. Plus, you have
> help you've never had before. Both changes can unhinge you.
> Here are the things that have helped me: First is painting, because
> that is something you can do yourself; it doesn't involve anybody
> else. Second, I love teaching, so I start to look into schools as soon
> as we get to a new place. But finding a teaching job doesn't
> happen overnight. It takes time; you have to find your way and
> make contacts. And I've made it a point never to have a full-time
> maid. It doesn't help you or your children to have somebody to do
> everything for you. In my experience, the person who has
> depended too much on externals, a mother, golf, or a bridge club,
> has the most trouble settling in.

An American physician stationed in West Germany reinforced these views. He said; "The happiest families are the
ones in which the mother has something to do. I encourage
mothers to try to get some kind of job even if they have small
children. Then they feel they are contributing something too,
and not just being a part of the party circuit."

All the Family

Everyone who has lived overseas emphasizes the importance of regularly setting aside time for family activities. One
teenager put it this way: "Don't worry about the museums and
the language, but impress upon the kids and their parents that
there should be more family solidarity."

Another adolescent stated this view in more detail:

> We've always done something each day together. My mother
> made a point of getting up at an unearthly hour just to eat with us
> before we went to school. When my father was home from his
> traveling we did one thing together, whether it was to play cards or
> just sit down and talk. And, when he could, he took us upcountry
> on his work.

Family Adjustments

A Foreign Service officer summarized family issues eloquently when he said:

> Most Foreign Service officers are aware of the necessity to deal with change, but they often get their family priorities mixed up with international ones. In other words, if the Foreign Service officer does not recognize that his highest priority is harmony in the family, he's in for trouble. And he's particularly vulnerable there, because he's also shooting for harmony in the world.

But none of the above dilemmas lacks a solution. The problems are nearly always surmountable; they need only be understood and then tackled with dispatch and wisdom.

"Train up a child in the way he should go. . . ."

—Proverbs, 22:6

VII

Child-Rearing Hints

EVERY CHILD grows up in observable and predictable phases of physical and emotional development that roughly correspond to chronological age. A parent who learns to recognize these characteristic thoughts and behaviors will be better able to handle the special concerns that inevitably arise in the course of a childhood spent abroad. A mother of three vigorous teenagers, all of whom had moved constantly throughout their lives, emphasized the point this way:

> Children can be raised successfully overseas, but it requires an awful lot of common sense and anticipation to minimize some of the bad parts. It's a matter of being informed about when to be easy on a child and when to be demanding, and it is amazing how many people are not. You must always think of the age of the child, because each age is going to bring up special problems overseas.

Before considering the special challenges of overseas living, let us summarize some basic characteristics of developmental stages so that you will have a map to identify just where you are when questions of discipline, feeding, or bedtime arise in your household. Some hints about developmental phases will supplement, but in no way substitute for, visits to a doctor or pediatrician. In addition, many excellent books on child-rearing are now available (see list at end of chapter). You may want to keep several books that concern your particular needs readily at hand. Books can indeed be helpful supports, particularly for mothers new to the game of child-rearing. Solutions can be found if a squalling four-month-old infant refuses to go to sleep or if one must introduce toilet training in a difficult living situation.

Childbirth

In the last part of pregnancy, a woman, particularly one having her first baby, often becomes preoccupied with her own body and the baby growing within her. Clothing for the infant and furniture and decorations for the baby's room take her time; thus, not much energy may be left for outside activities or even for her husband. She is a vulnerable person, uncertain about how attractive she is in her new state. A pregnant wife needs to be assured that she is important to her husband despite the changes of her physical contours.

Before and immediately at childbirth, mothers focus all their attention on the new life around them, and husbands may feel somewhat left out. It is at this very period that family difficulties may develop if a father suddenly thinks he is no longer important and, therefore, turns to his work or other interests to fill the void. The whole period surrounding pregnancy is one in which both mother and father should allot time to spend at home, with enough free hours to be together.

It is certainly not the moment for traveling, entertaining, or taking on extra job pressures. A new mother and her baby need good and consistent care. And husbands can help by being *available*, fending off extra social obligations and participating in the planning of the life of the new baby.

Overseas Hints

A husband might use his familiarity with a foreign country when it is time to choose an obstetrician and a maternity hospital. He can visit the hospital before his wife's admission so that when the crucial hours of labor and delivery arrive all the procedures will go smoothly. He may perhaps call a friend who speaks the host country language and ask him to be present during the crucial hospital admission procedures. When a complicated delivery is anticipated because of medical problems, it becomes doubly important that all the details of physicians, hospitalization, and later care of both mother and infant go smoothly.

An enthusiastic baby nurse can be a welcome blessing to a tired mother, although one should keep in mind that the arrival of another woman into a household sets the stage for an inevitable negotiation, if not a battle, about who is going to be in charge of the baby. Painful situations can develop, and mothers may retire from such battles in depressed and puzzled defeat. The problems become compounded when a new mother in a new country and a new culture holds old uncertainties from her relationship with her own mother. Defeats and even the battles themselves can be avoided if the mother stakes out important areas of a baby's care—fixing the formula, bathing, playtimes—as her own (chap. 8).

Hotel living is a trying experience at any time, but the sterility of a hotel room is particularly oppressive to a mother with a newborn infant. A concerned husband will do everything he can to make a hotel room as homelike as possible in order to counteract its sometimes austere and unpleasant qualities. The hotel management will have no objections if a family brings its own blankets, puts up a mobile over the infant's bed, and finds a few simple toys. You can make a part of the room, which should be out of noisy or bewildering lobbies and dining rooms, a "nest" where you feed and play with the baby. Some families have found that the simple expedient of moving furniture around in their rooms makes the barren atmosphere more homelike. A radio, some family pictures, and a few familiar paintings all will add warm touches.

Infancy (Birth to One Year of Age)

In order to develop a sense of predictability in his life, an infant needs to be fed, kept warm, changed, and offered stimulation by a dependable person who effectively takes care of his needs. The infant develops an ability to recognize hunger and its satisfaction through his daily interactions with his mother; he becomes confident that his rhythms of sleeping, feeding, and elimination will be met in a reliable and pleasing way, and, in the course of all these experiences, he develops an intense and trusting attachment to his mother. Though these rhythms seem to be imposed by the parent, the process is, in fact, a mutual one of give and take between adult and infant. The latter not only is molded by his mother but also molds the form of the mutual interaction he and his mother develop.

The young infant is exceedingly aware of his environment and benefits from the reliability of his mother. He is comforted by living in a place he recognizes, surrounded by his toys and a level of sound that is regular and comforting. Since the attachment he makes to his mother is one of the most intense of his life, and will be a touchstone for all later attachments, it is vital that it be a good one.

Overseas Hints

A wise mother will fill as many of her baby's needs and activities as her energy and interests allow. Mother's helpers and nursemaids can be useful, but it is the mother who makes the decisions so that her newborn learns to trust her and identify with her. Budget a healthy period of time during which you remain at home with your small child, and take him with you when you go out. At the same time, small children also need practice in being on their own so that they can develop a sense of security. Both babies and mothers profit from reasonably dosed times away from each other.

Infants from six months to one year of age do not readily accept strangers. Many babies go through a period of several months in which they show "stranger anxiety"—that is, crying, irritability, or discomfort when persons other than their mothers hold or feed them. Therefore, it is wise to protect infants who experience such anxiety from hordes of adults who want to hold or cuddle them, even though an American mother may be tempted to use an infant as a means of encouraging host country adults to relate to her family.

One-to-Three-Year-Olds

The toddler is an explorer. He vigorously studies his body and then all the world around him. Territoriality and possessions are important to him; he gets into everything he can and roams widely if permitted to do so; he begins to name things and to master his first learned language. This period is often called one of muscular control because one-to-three-year-olds naturally direct themselves to harnessing their muscular energy in organized activity.

The young toddler tries to define his abilities and his boundaries. He will push a caretaker, pull at her dress, or take things from her. His great energy goes into toddling and imposing his will on the outside world. A great deal of negative feeling may come out in the form of crying, tantrums, and rages when he overshoots his goals or loses control of his body.

Toilet training illustrates his concern with compliance and opposition. The toddler holds things in or spurts them out in a haphazard fashion that may be in conflict with a caretaker's attempts to make him more regular.

Overseas Hints

Experienced mothers provide the toddler with as much room as possible. They allow him to climb, kick, throw objects, feed himself, and get dirty—within acceptable limits. Nursemaids sometimes are dominated by an energetic, demanding child and give in to his wishes far too much. The result will be an overstimulated and overgratified child with little sense of limits. Conversely, a household helper may so supress a toddler's natural exuberance that he will never have a chance to test out his muscles and learn limits to his behavior. Overgratification will result in a combative, uncontrolled child; conversely, inhibition of activity will result in an overly neat, submissive, and docile youngster.

Personal possessions and toys are important. These help to establish a child's place in the world and also provide him with a way to develop his capabilities. American manufacturers have devised rugged toys of particular developmental relevance for the toddler and preschooler. Blocks, patterns, moving items, and objects that can be manipulated are classics of American ingenuity marketed by such well-known companies as Playskool, Creative Play Things, and Child Craft. Some of these products may be available in certain foreign countries. At the same time, a child needs a stick and a rag from which he can make a doll and some simple blocks of wood that he can transform into a castle. Leave a space and provide materials for fantasy play and free your child of the need to depend exclusively on manufactured materials.

Regular bedtime habits help to control the frequent fears of the dark and worries about noise and separation that fester unless dealt with carefully. Put your child to bed yourself, at the same time each night, with a familiar story in a quiet atmosphere and he will sleep well and thank you a thousand times as he grows older (chap. 12).

Three-to-Six-Year-Olds

Physical boyishness and girlishness predominate during this period. Many girls assert their femininity by the development of a consuming interest in bathing, combing their hair, or adorning their bodies. They love to prance around in new clothes and, by twirling and dancing, show how pretty they are. Girls may become unusually motherly at this period or demonstrate a pronounced curiosity about their genital areas. Boys typically swagger and strut about in defiant ways and draw attention to their physical strength. Fights at home and free-for-alls in school attest to their concern with their bodies. They often become preoccupied with their genitals. This is the time when children play "doctor" and explore each other's nakedness behind closed bathroom doors.

Child-Rearing Hints

Because three-to-six-year-olds polarize their attitudes toward their parents, this has also been dubbed the Oedipal period. Boys want to emulate their fathers in every way—dress like them, talk like them, be like them. But a parent also must be prepared to accept some defiance and criticism from an Oedipal son. Indeed, a boy's feelings toward his father will contain a mixture of admiration and a certain amount of competitiveness.

A girl's situation at this period is in some ways a simpler one; she will want to become like her mother. This identification may well lead her to care for younger siblings and assist with cooking and housework. A girl needs an opportunity to see her mother and other women in fulfilling roles that give them a sense of significance. Nursemaids and other helpers must demonstrate a positive sense of their own identity so that children can relate to them in a warm, respectful, and happy way. It should be remembered that an overemphasis on pretty dresses or voice inflections may convince children that only external prettiness or an authoritative voice is desirable to parents. Children need to become like their parents, but they need to become what they are capable of being even more. The understanding of these problems may, therefore, be of great importance in deciding the fate of a child's character development.

In order to want to become like her mother, a girl must have a strong and effective mother to copy. She will dress and walk like the woman closest to her. But the country in which they live also helps mold American girls overseas. They will imitate the fashions and respond to the fears and excitements around them because they are so involved with fantasy at this age. Young girls may, in fact, worry about being kidnapped, carried off by jinns, sold into slavery, or snatched away by gypsies.

If girls are valued only as sex objects in a society, it will be difficult for them to grow up to become mature adults. When menses are considered to be "dirty," pregnancy ugly, and child-rearing an unimportant activity, a growing girl is bound to be influenced by such views. Parents can counteract the unfortunate devaluation of women in many countries by educating their daughters and by encouraging the caretakers to instil positive values. The development of healthy attitudes toward womanhood become especially important in Asia and Africa. Since it has become more complicated to define healthy feminine attitudes because of the great effect of the contemporary feminist movement in the United States, women and girls living overseas would do well to keep abreast of these concerns so that they and all of their family will be able to fit in comfortably when they return stateside to live.

It is easier for a boy to step down from the pedestal of chauvinistic over-valuation, which is a male privilege in many countries, than it is for a girl to climb out of the sink hole into which she may have been placed. Still, boys profit from realistic assessments of their position in a family and a society. A father can help his son separate the special sexual views and mores of a country in which they live from those views held by their own family.

How about sexuality? It is not a good idea to let children sleep in the same room with their caretakers because of the resulting over-stimulation. You can guard a child against sexual experiences that he might witness in a maid's house by explicitly discussing such potential issues with the household helper. Male caretakers show particular difficulty in dealing with children, for they are complicated identification figures and often, even unwittingly, over-stimulate the young they care for.

The three-to-six-year-old, fighting the battle for independence from his parents, has a particularly difficult time with manners. He will do the opposite of what his mother and father request in order to get some attention. He will talk back to his parents, use four-letter words, interrupt conversations, place his foot in the nose of a visiting dignitary at home, and get into fights at school. This is the natural result of the child's attempt to become a little more independent. Parents need to consider how much naughtiness and rebellion they will tolerate and then decide on reasonable limits to such behavior.

A parent can figure out how much of a child's defiance requires firmer controls and how much reflects a need for more attention. Sometimes youngsters will seek attention by being "bad" in ways that threaten to influence a parent's career. A child's behavior—even fire-setting or drug use in an older youngster—should never be sufficient cause for the termination of a parent's job and a return to the United States. Heads of organizations should keep this point in mind so that parents are not tyrannized by the disturbed behavior of their children.

Seven-to-Eleven-Year-Olds

From age seven and into the beginning of adolescence, a young person ordinarily lives through a relatively tranquil time when he can focus his attention on learning. He no longer is so preoccupied with a need to be loved or with his passionate commitments to his father or mother. Instead, he can concentrate on the pleasures of manipulating numbers and the satisfaction of mastering concepts. He begins to read for his own pleasure and pursues hobbies because they capture his imagination. The child of this age shows a true love of rules—the rules of games, of grammar, of arithmetic. He works with an increasing concern for precision and becomes upset when projects don't turn out exactly as he planned them. He rarely looks to his parents for guidance but, instead, depends upon himself and his teachers, and begins to blame himself when things don't turn out well. As he moves from his parent-centered world, he falls into a group-centered world. Children of this age show a slavish adherence to group pressures and group expectations. They choose a leader and follow his wishes explicitly. Clubs and gangs begin to flourish, and conformity to others in a gang is highly valued.

Since ages seven to eleven are the time for the educational process to take hold, a child's school experience should be stable, serene, and safe. It is unwise to overwhelm children with too many trips, disruptions, or moves from house to house. When moves are necessary, they must be planned with great care (chap. 4).

Parents should support a child's school and his teachers. Criticism of teachers or a school undermines a child's identification with the education process. Don't compete with your child's school by offering more alluring enticements at home, for an over-gratified youngster will find it difficult to leave home and make his way on his own (chap. 9).

Parents also should be careful not to criticize each other openly, complain about the maid, or devalue host country nationals within earshot of children. A child who hears criticism of others will believe that at least a part of it is aimed at him.

Adolescence

The teenager wants to be on his own as much as possible. He prefers to choose his own clothes, his own friends, his own activities. Unless he is given scope to develop a reasonable life of his own, he may rebel against rules and cause trouble in the community. He has a tougher row to hoe overseas because adolescence is a difficult and precarious time wherever a person may grow up. Adolescents new to a community must tread carefully and depend upon the counseling of their parents as they choose their friends. As one teenager put it:

> When you're new in a place, you want to become assimilated and you want to make it with the other kids. That's why drugs are so important. Kids in the drug scene are the ones that will approach you first, but then you get caught in their ways. They dress differently; they are always skipping school; they don't do well in school and don't want to.

The teenager, with one foot in the security of childhood and one in the choices of adult life, and often poised between marking time overseas and preparing to plunge into the youth society of the United States, needs special attention. Because adolescence is the most trying developmental period overseas for teenager and parent alike, all of chapter 10 is devoted to it.

Friends

Friendships make all the difference between a happy adjustment to a post and a disastrous one. School difficulties and troubles at home often can be traced to a lack of solid friendship, whereas fond recollections of overseas life are based on the buddies and pals a child recalls. Parents can help a youngster initiate friendships. It is fortunate that the built-in responsiveness of the small, transient, and interdependent American communities overseas favors the acceptance of newcomers.

The first days at a post are crucial for initiating friendships; special efforts made then will pay off handsomely. Some parents arrange an outing that includes several of their children's schoolmates; thoughtful mothers invite children home for lunch and playtime. The community swimming pool and crafts groups are natural gathering points for making friends. Since young children feel most comfortable when their own parents know and like their friends' parents, invitations for a shared family dinner, picnic, or group volleyball game can help youngsters become members of the gang in their school.

Relationships with host country nationals add special complications to the question of friendship. Here are some examples of the great variety of ways in which children and families become involved with host country children:

First all the children would begin to play together, Americans, Egyptians, Israelis, Germans, Ethiopians, you name it. Then parents started inviting each other back and forth, and pretty soon all these people who are supposed to be enemies had become fast friends.

I wanted my children to play with children of all kinds. My landlord warned me against letting my youngsters associate with what he called "those dirty street urchins," but I was full of the brotherhood of man until my son was buried and sealed in a hole by those very children while they were playing football. When I found him, I changed my tune and explained to him that, until we had been here a while, it would be better for him to play on the school grounds and recognize that not everybody in the country was necessarily his friend.

Our children were outside having a snowball fight with some Yugoslav youngsters. The fight got out of hand and ended with bruised tempers and three broken windows in our house. I then marched out and pinned a note on our wall saying, "we are still your friends but you can't play so rough." The next day our doorbell rang and there were six Yugoslav kids who came to apologize. One said, "My mother told me we had to apologize and be friendly because you were good foreigners."

I played games with some of the Russian kids occasionally and we had some bad experiences with them. For example, you can't buy chewing gum easily in Russia. The Russian kids used to bully us to get chewing gum because we got it from the commissary and then they wouldn't be friendly with you again if you didn't keep on giving them gum.

Try to keep an even perspective in regard to friendships with host country children, and remember that bullying and intimidation are not unknown in the United States. Happily, many difficult situations end in warm friendships. Some efforts on your part will assist children to spot the kind of host country youngsters they can enjoy despite differing value orientations.

Languages

It cannot be said fairly that Americans show a fondness for foreign languages. Though many nationals of other nations speak English, new overseas American families may be in for a surprise, especially those who choose to integrate the fabric of a host country by living away from Army bases or outside the American "ghettos." An apartment in Paris or a little house in a Danish village will necessitate the acquisition of a second language.

American children, like all children, are *naturally* bilingual. They learn rapidly. Six weeks spent at a German *kinderheim* near Stuttgart can be enough; when the traveling American parents return to pick up their three-year-old, Johnny will babble in fluent German, complete with local Swabian dialect. (At the same time, young Johnny may have lost much of his English during the six weeks.) In some American homes on foreign soil, the parents may be so busy that the local Spanish or Portuguese or Japanese maid will take over; as result, even the smallest tot learns one of these tongues.

Although psychological research has not clearly established

whether it is better for a child to learn one or several languages in infancy, it is quite clear that unless you participate in his learning a toddler may end up speaking the tongue of the host country and not that of his parents. "My brother and I spoke German first, because we learned from our maids," a teenager recalled. "We talked in German to the maid and to each other and then translated to our parents, who did not speak the language. It created a real gap between us and our mother and father." If you can't keep up with your youngster, be sure that you reinforce his English so that you can talk to your own child and not have to converse with him through a translator.

There are some excellent bilingual schools abroad, particularly in Paris, Geneva, Rome, West Berlin, and Cairo, where native teachers insure that American youngsters do equally well in two tongues. A parent may consider whether or not the second language may prove useful in the young person's future; if so, the international instead of American overseas schools prove worthwhile.

When a foreign language is added merely as an ornament, or because of a parent's wish rather than a real need for it, stormy scenes may ensue. If your child tries to learn a second language, help him to learn it by your own use of it at home to show interest in his progress.

It is true that there are some extremely difficult and rare tongues that would take up an inordinate amount of study time to learn, only to be discarded after a year's tour of duty in India or Afghanistan or Zambia. The situation changes for the expatriate, however. For the overseas American, the effort may become important. In this respect, it is interesting to note that new language learning systems have become sophisticated enough for the Peace Corps, for example, to teach trainees the most complex Indian dialects by means of "crash" courses. Teenage children can utilize the same learning systems.

Some Americans who work overseas for long periods of time

prefer to place their children in schools of the host country. One graduate of such an experience recalled it this way:

> It was an extraordinary time. We learned four languages at once, practicing them through films, plays, and conversation. The faculty changed each day's language. On Monday it might be French at meals, the next day meant German conversation, and so on. I still speak all four languages well and translate professionally in two.

The above description doesn't concern every American family, of course, so be sure that your child learns one language well! In consultation with his teachers, help him with sentence structure and synonyms so that he will feel secure in his use of language. Give him opportunities to use his language skills without embarrassment.

A Final Word About Development Stages

In each stage of development, a child is molded by the way his parents respond to parallel developmental issues in their own lives. The infant living in a magical world of total bliss or overwhelming fear needs parents who do not panic at real danger or lose themselves in an oblivion of evasion and denial. The muscular, domineering toddler needs parents who delight in energetic, active pursuits. The sexual curiosity of a five-year-old must be met by healthy acceptance and respect for sexuality on the part of his parents. Some general psychiatric principles will help children through each developmental phase: raising children takes time, a lot of it. Both mothers and fathers need to budget a block of their time if they expect to have psychologically healthy children. Overseas parents who retain the primary responsibility for their offspring will get love and trust from them in return. Conversely, parents whose young were cared for exclusively by outsiders will have children who feel rejected. No matter how much a "nanny" cherishes and loves Johnny, that child will feel devalued because his parents were willing to give him up to a caretaker. Underneath Johnny's anger will be his feeling that he was abandoned by parents who allowed him to be taken over entirely by someone else.

Both boys and girls need time with both parents and with each parent alone. This helps them to identify with their elders in the complex and varied ways that define maleness and femaleness. There is no way to evade this obvious truth, though many overseas families have tried.

—Children need lots of love. The expression of a parent's love will change from the cuddling and peek-a-boo games of infancy to shared walks and conversation with a ten-year-old, but intimate, loving involvement remains a steady necessity throughout childhood. A harassed father should leave thoughts of international crises at his office when he converses or plays with his offspring.

—Planning and regularity will prepare children to accept and master the inevitable troubles and uncertainties of a transient overseas life.

—Awareness is needed of the specific demands and tensions that surface with each developmental stage. At the same time, sensitivity to individual differences pays dividends. Allow for leeway in a child's behavior when he has just moved, including a tolerant attitude toward lapses in manners. Each child is an individual and will grow according to his own schedule rather than one defined in a book.

—Support a child's strengths and ignore or minimize weaknesses whenever possible. As a result, a child will learn to feel good about himself. A philosophical track coach illustrated this principle with the following story. He observed the running form of one of his charges and then said to him, "Your starts are lousy but your turns are excellent." The runner expected to be told to work on his starts, but instead the coach said laconically, "Practice your turns and you'll be a fine runner." The same advice applies to the rearing of children. Identify their strengths and maximize them.

—Overseas children must learn to get along without the unconditional love and extravagant admiration of grandparents, just as overseas parents must do without the support of their own mothers and fathers. Though no exact prescription can make up for this deprivation, ingenious parents have found surrogate grandparents for their children or arranged for visits home to make up for the loss.

—Develop a point of view about maids, cooks, and caretakers so that your children can take their cue from you. Is a maid a peer who happens to do housework in your home or is she someone who takes your place? Is the German scrubwoman a person to be criticized openly, a kind of devalued woman who bears all the burden of the "woman's role" through the ages? Is a nursemaid or governess the secret "mother" of a child?

—Define limits of behavior exactly and simply as soon as you get to a new post. Tell children how far they can roam in a new town, when they must check in, what is safe and what is dangerous.

—In order for a youngster to feel good about himself, his parents and the community around him must approve of his behavior; that is, they must appreciate the infant who wants to be hugged and held, the toddler who manifests a delight in manipulating the environment, the five-year-old who demonstrates his strength or masculinity. Self-esteem is important. The community in which a child lives must also approve of the healthy scuffling of one child as well as the charming seductiveness of another.

All of these ideas about raising children cluster around the concepts of development stages. If you know where your child fits developmentally, you then can aid him to deal effectively with the special characteristics of childhood overseas. You might want to refer to some of the books listed below to fill out your knowledge of the developmental needs of all children.

Useful Books on Child-Rearing

American Academy of Pediatrics, *Standards of Child Health Care* (1972). P.O. Box 1034, Evanston, Illinois 60204. Excellent listings of books and pamphlets for parents on specific diseases and health needs of children.
Brazelton, T., *Toddlers and Parents* (New York: Delacorte Press, 1975).
Fraiberg, Selma, *The Magic Years* (New York: Scribners, 1959).
Gregg, Elizabeth, *What To Do When "There's Nothing To Do"* (New York: Delacorte Press, 1968). Divided by ages; gives materials and directions for the activities.
Johnson, June, *838 Ways To Amuse A Child* (Riverside, New Jersey: Macmillan, 1970).
Spock, Benjamin, *Baby and Child Care* (New York: Pocket Books, 1968).
Spock, Benjamin, *A Teenager's Guide To Life and Love* (New York: Pocket Books, 1971).

VIII

"We were adored and entertained every day of our idyllic young lives in India by a whole procession of native servants who wanted nothing more than to delight us, beguile us, and bewitch us.
—A woman raised overseas

Another Mother: The Child Caretaker

THIS KIPLINGESQUE vision of an overseas world is well and good, but if you are the mother of such adored and beguiled children, you must make a series of decisions and determine priorities to help you steer a sensible course for your children, your entire family, and the people who work for you.

The American family overseas must first decide whether substitute mothers are needed at all or whether it is better to get along without them. Some Americans have found that a household is simpler to manage without outside help. With no governess to get between them, a mother and her children will know exactly where they stand with each other, and the mother certainly will have a defined job as her overseas life begins. Those parents who decide to employ helpers in their house should ask themselves whether they want them to do solely the washing, housework, and marketing or to be caretakers for their children. Unless clear decisions about these matters are made at the start of employment, everyone will be confused about who is in charge of what. Although the many issues involved in employing cooks, cleaning women, nursemaids, and sweepers could fill a course in industrial psychology, let us concentrate on the one main issue of children and how they and their parents relate to caretakers.

In the process of moving overseas where child care is readily available, even to families of modest means, a youngster may become a pawn in an inadvertent trade of mothers. The lower the age, the more permanent may be the impact of the trade. In such a trade, the child gains not only a built-in playmate and nursemaid but also the values, habits, and fears she brings; a mother may gain free time but, in the process, may lose a certain intensity of relationship with her children. As one overseas-reared adult recalled, "All my deepest love, greatest loyalties, and fondest memories are centered on my *aya* and not my mother." Parents who dilute their responsibilities with a nursemaid in the United States complicate their children's development, but the idiosyncratic child-care practices of other countries add a special element to the growth of children. Unless the whole process is thought out carefully, children will grow up with fragmented loyalties and ingrained habits that will be difficult to modify. Entire families may find their bonds of intimacy replaced by tangled strands of guilt, estrangement, and resentment.

These may be chilling diagnoses and predictions; they are important enough to deserve to be considered in detail. Ways to avert many of these problems can be found, along with answers to those that are inevitable. But planning, flexibility, and constant hard work are necessary to provide solutions.

Since most Americans in the United States either cannot or choose not to hire help, the overseas situation poses a unique problem. A major change of attitude is necessary when there is little alternative to the employment of caretakers. And there is, in fact, little alternative in countries that do not have supermarkets, electric stoves, washing machines or cooperative child-care facilities, but do possess an abundance of prohibitions and time-consuming customs.

Often a family moves overseas to a new job, new customs, a new language, and a company policy that a cook, housekeeper, and child caretaker come with the house. Many mothers delight in such a prospect but then find themselves sliding down into a vortex of complicated rules, involvements, and concerns between themselves, their children, and their caretakers. Even those who wish to care for their children themselves frequently find that the initial blast of social activity overseas changes their minds. A mother recalled just such a situation: "The very first thing that happened when we arrived was that we were expected to jump into a round of our predecessor's going away parties. That meant we were out five nights in a row, leaving screaming and disorganized little ones in the hands of a different person each night. I gave in very quickly and hired a nursemaid."

Finding a Good Caretaker

Most communities have a ready supply of nursemaids, variously called nannies, *ayas*, or *amas*, who have worked for American families and are handed down from one family to another. Even when you are presented with someone who "comes with the house," such a person can be molded to meet your needs if you are willing to become a combination employer, adviser, friend, cajoler, and child psychologist. Before you make a final decision, scour your community to discover the person who will best fit your family's needs.

Desirable Personality Traits

The best way to learn about a child caretaker is to observe her with your children. Take her with you on an outing, a picnic, or a visit and see how she fits in with your offspring and your family. Does she play with them and help them only when they need nelp? Does she help you? How does she interact with people you meet along the way? Decide whether her personality traits and habits mesh with your youngsters' needs and your wishes.

Obviously, caretakers who are tolerant and self-confident, who enjoy children and show affection with them, would be most desirable. Energy and a sense of real playfulness and pleasure over childlike activities are most important. If you can do so, guard against the person who overwhelms children with attention and concern.

Age

Choose a caretaker who is either sixteen to twenty-four years of age, or perhaps 35 years or older. A young girl still has a great deal of free energy, usually is eager to please, and wants to learn from a family. She will still look forward to her marriage and her own children and won't overly invest in your children and find herself, even unconsciously, attempting to put herself between them and you. Great practical experience need not be a critical issue in your choice, since many girls overseas have already looked after younger siblings in their own homes. Rather, what you need to look for is a sense of spontaneity and real joy shown with your own children.

Older women who have already had their own children can also make extremely capable caretakers. They know the ropes, what should be expected of youngsters, and tend to be firm with them. Older, experienced, married women caretakers are ideal because, like young, unmarried girls, they do not become overly possessive with children.

Women who have no children or only a single child are more of a gamble. Limited experience results in a limited base of judgment. All mothers will tell you that they wish they had known when they had their first-born what they learned after their third or fourth child had grown up. The same is true with caretakers, and, in the usual buyer's market that you find overseas, you will have the opportunity to choose someone who fits your needs well.

If there is any caretaker to be wary of, it is the middle-aged woman who has never married. Although such a person can be excellent at her job, she often is so caught up in her own feelings of loneliness and childlessness that she will overly invest in your children and, in effect, steal them away from you, even though she has no conscious intention of doing so.

Her Family

We employed a nanny who said that her daughter would cook and help take care of our three children. I then found that nanny had a husband, four young children, and a mother who expected to move into a little shack on our land. By the time we took stock, we had not only a group of caretakers but also a whole clan of their Tolstoyan relatives living in our compound.

Because it is only too easy to stumble into sticky situations such as the one described above, a family must state the terms of the work contract in careful detail when first employing help. It is smart to seek advice from experienced people in your community about acceptable guidelines for living arrangements, pay, time off, food, clothing, and relatives. This way one can avoid the development of misunderstandings and dissatisfaction.

Families differ greatly on how much egalitarian interaction

they wish to have between their own children and the children of their hired help. The issue will arise, however, and needs to be faced head-on, or trouble may ensue. One woman echoed the sentiments of many when she said:

> I don't think it is a good practice to let your children play regularly with the caretaker's children. There will be problems with theft because children who have nothing are certainly going to pick up toys, balls, and other things like that. You have problems with dirt and, perhaps, even homosexual practices. These servants' kids coming in and out of the house make life very complicated since their ways are so different from the ones we want our children to have.

This somewhat harsh statement is in some cases not unrealistic.

The Mother-Caretaker Relationship

There is a narrow line between giving up your child to a nursemaid and not giving the nursemaid enough freedom in the care of your child. If you want your child dressed in a particular fashion, set out his clothes yourself each day. Do not encourage a nursemaid to dress him and then criticize her choice of clothes. Tell your child's caretaker what you expect of her, almost as a drill sergeant would command his troops. At the same time, you will want her friendship and cheerful willingness to cooperate with you in the rearing of your children. A caretaker will be infinitely more comfortable if she knows that a mother wants her child's face and hands washed before each meal and her room tidied up by the child at a regular time.

Pampering

A parent should be clear about preferred child-rearing principles and be definite with caretakers about them. Once a mother has given responsibility to a caretaker, she must back up the employee in dealing with a child. It is not necessary to snoop a great deal, or to ignore the children entirely. In many countries, issues such as cleanliness, sexuality, and sleeping arrangements need particular attention from mothers. Some issues can easily be observed, and others have to be anticipated and ferreted out. Extreme pampering is a typical situation to be encountered. Because caretakers depend upon their jobs, they will go to great lengths to keep a child smiling and satisfied. They want to make sure that a child does not cry or become upset in any way, and the easiest way to keep a child pacified is to rock him, sing to him, and feed him or sleep with him. Children need to develop autonomy but can't do so if caretakers constantly fuss and fret over them and satisfy every whim almost before it is expressed.

Overprotectiveness

Overprotectiveness is another dilemma. One mother described it this way:

> The main problems with having nannies is that they become absolutely horrified that something is going to happen to a child in their care. Therefore, they become overprotective in order to keep their jobs, and you can't blame them for that. For example, since I raised five children in the United States before I went overseas, I knew that children will climb trees and even fall out of them at times. That's the way they learn. I never worried at home unless there was actually blood on the scene. So my children developed a very strong "I can do it" attitude, which is really the heart of the American approach anyway. A child raised by an *aya* will not have this self-confidence. Instead, when caretakers are afraid to discipline kids, you end up with spoiled brats who are afraid to do anything for themselves.

In Thailand a nursemaid frequently cradles an infant or young child in her arms wherever she goes. The child is picked up out of bed in the morning, sits in the nursemaid's

95

lap during breakfast, and is carried around during chores or activities. The child is always played with, protected, and cared for. He rarely gets the opportunity to be alone, try his wings, have accidents, or learn by experience. Instead, even at the age of four, many children in this culture are fearful of moving about; they hover around their nursemaids and remain sweet-tempered and unaggressive. These may be adaptive traits for a Thai child, for he has other experiences later in life that tend to counteract this overprotectiveness. However, the American youngsters brought back to the more turbulent American scene at school age may be extremely dependent and fearful children, uncomfortable with the active, rough-and-tumble ways of their peers.

Since children reared by nursemaids may feel particularly insecure and fearful, a mother might work to counteract such feelings by setting herself the tasks of encouraging responsibility, autonomy, and an ability to cope with new situations. You might insist that a child clean his room, choose his own clothes, and help with the shopping in order to balance the inevitable pampering he will receive from a nursemaid.

Food

Caretakers generally believe that a fat child is a healthy child, and many caretakers who cook do so with heavy cream, butter, oil, and lard. In some countries, American children, therefore, develop objectionable eating habits and fat stomachs under the tutelage of a nanny. It takes subtle negotiation to change the ways of a child's beloved nursemaid who, as a mother recalled, "got terribly upset if my son didn't want to have three rolls, four glasses of juice, and a pound of butter every morning for breakfast."

Another Mother: The Child Caretaker

Mothers and Fathers

Prepare yourself for some change in your children's attitudes toward you when a caretaker enters your house. If she feeds your children and plays with them much of their free time, they may well turn to her for the warmth and coziness they need and view their actual mother as a "bad" person, who appears in their lives only to question, correct, or spank them. Try not to feel devastated if a child rebuffs you. Instead, you might say, "You must feel hurt that I spend less time with you since Nanny came. I'm glad you care so much for Nanny, but I still love you as much as ever." Nevertheless, you will probably note some difference in your attitude toward your children and they may note a similar change in their feelings toward you. As one child raised by a child caretaker recalled. "If you're brought up by servants, you are just less dependent on your parents. It's that simple."

"For his first five years, our youngest child grew up with an Urdu-speaking *aya*," a mother recalled. "They were inseparable, and my son spoke Urdu far better than he did English. He never could communicate with my husband, who rarely knew what our son was talking about. Endless frustration resulted from that." Language problems are compounded further when caretakers and children band together to share secrets in a language neither parent can understand. Such situations should stimulate parents to try to learn the native language.

To prevent misunderstandings, parents would do well to work out between themselves a mutually agreed-upon policy concerning a caretaker's responsibilities. One father recalled this about his wife and himself:

We sometimes countermand each other's orders. Should the maid sweep, put a table in one place or another? I feel that if there is something I can do, I'm not going to ask somebody else to do it, but my wife doesn't feel that way. I don't want outside help coming around to turn on the lights all the time or open doors for me. My wife does, and the children pick up things from her.

Children can be surly to baby-sitters and then become surly to adults whom they think they can boss around. Parents must be alert to such difficulties and work to minimize them.

Adults and Caretakers

An adult's attitude toward caretakers will mold a child's attitude. As one parent recalled:

Some people are too authoritarian and they don't give any respect to maids; others are too lenient and don't get any respect from servants. We Americans are just not used to having servants and find ourselves all mixed up when we're with them. Children pick this up. It's tough to hit a median. For example, when children go to the movies and see our nanny there, the nanny will bow and scrape before them. The children then get used to ordering the help around and end up doing the same thing with teachers, other adults, everybody.

In brief, a stand-in mother should be treated with dignity by the entire family. The proper respect and a slight distance are better than total intimacy, which, in the end, only breeds contempt. For this reason, an American mother need not burden her children's Thai caretaker with her worries, marital problems, confidences, or uncertainties. Most women who become caretakers of children overseas do not have the vision or education to deal effectively with such American concerns. When asked to do so, they lose a sense of perspective about their employer. Though a mother may be disappointed by the lack of closeness that results from such a structured arrangement, it will simplify a family's life.

It may not seem possible to those of you whose hired hands are old, gnarled, and wizened creatures, but even seduction may enter the picture. As one knowledgeable teenager recalled, "A hopeless problem develops when a maid who is a pretty young girl seduces your father in your own house. Then she has the whole family at ransom for three or four years with no one knowing exactly where he stands."

Sleeping Arrangements

After babyhood, children deserve to have their own rooms or to sleep in a room with a sibling. It is both over-stimulating and disturbing for a child to share the bedroom of an adult, because the child comes to depend upon the presence of the adult to help him fall asleep. Do not encourage a child's caretaker to fall into the practice of sleeping with him, although such arrangements may be known in many countries. The situation is the seedbed of all kinds of subsequent problems. For example, one child feared sleeping with his windows open for years because an *aya*, who shared his room, told him bats would fly in at night and suck their blood if the windows were even cracked. (Chapters 7 and 12 cover these issues in detail.)

The Sick Child

Illness may bring out irrational and overprotective responses in all of us, but a nursemaid with little education and mystifying theories of illness can thwart sensible treatment of a sick child. When giving medicine, she may decide that, if a little is useful, more would be better and, in the process, overdose a sick child. She may encourage an overlong convalescence out of her protective wishes. Or she may offer folk remedies that complicate a child's recovery.

One mother described such a situation to me:

When we first went to Turkey, Christopher got sick with a high fever. In the little town we lived in, calling the doctor was a great

99

event you didn't indulge in until the moment of death was at hand. Our maid said she could cure Christopher, so she started by rubbing eucalyptus oil on his chest. She bathed him all over in vinegar and put pieces of cold meat on his wrists and ankles to bring his fever down, at which point he looked like a damned salad. So I said, "To hell with this," and called the doctor, who came and prescribed nine different medicines, which turned out to be too much for the child. We finally reached a competent doctor, but no more home remedies for me. (See chapter 13.)

Travel

Parents develop great confidence in caretakers and sometimes decide to leave their children alone with them. Rarely does this work out well, especially with a young foreign baby-sitter, since her own judgment and impulse control are often imperfectly formed. This case example from my practice will illustrate the problems.

A ten-year-old girl, whom we will call Carol, came to me because of unusual fearfulness and depression, which had developed in the previous year. The first nine years of her life were spent in the Middle East under the care of a young nursemaid. Though Carol grew well in many ways, she sucked her thumb constantly. The nursemaid accepted and even encouraged this behavior, which she repeatedly said was comforting to a child. Carol's mother disapproved of the thumbsucking, but her opinion was overruled by the nurse-maid, who had far more experience in caring for children.

When Carol was nine, her parents, secure in their trust of the nursemaid, who had been with them for seven years, went away on a three-week trip and left Carol and her younger brother in the total charge of the nursemaid. The parents returned from their trip to find their daughter and her younger brother overwrought and full of fears. Carol, particularly, asked that her parents stay with her, refused to go out and visit other houses, and continued to be extremely uncomfortable about being alone for an entire year following her parents' single trip. She complained in a cryptic way that "Alkisti locked the door." The parents questioned the nursemaid about the matter but never learned anything of substance, and Carol never explained things further.

Not until the end of the tour did the parents learn, by a complicated coincidence, that the nursemaid's boyfriend had moved into the house during the absence of the parents. During this period, Alkisti, previously an open, warm person, locked the children's bedroom doors when they went to sleep. She then furtively brought her boyfriend into the house and, when the children learned about this, swore them both to secrecy about the events under pain of terrible punishment and loss of love.

Carol was frightened and perplexed by the experience; such an experience is simply too stimulating for a young child to integrate and inevitably results in discomfort and confusion on the part of the child.

Needless to say, the above is an isolated experience. But it could happen. It is unwise to leave children alone for long periods of time in the charge of caretakers, especially if they are new. Moreover, young caretakers, no matter how devoted they may be, may become entangled in situations in which they lose control, particularly in male-dominated countries. Parents who travel a great deal should first get thoroughly acquainted with baby-sitters and nursemaids. When the local sitter is still an unknown quantity, be certain that a responsible adult looks in on the children and talks with them regularly and candidly.

Sex

Young children need someone to mother them, to cuddle, hold, and rock them. All of these healthy, stimulating activities, plus diaper changing and bathing, are best handled by

101

women, yet many countries have a tradition that includes the use of male child caretakers. Expert opinions vary regarding that tradition. Though I am sure some men can do an excellent, safe job of raising babies, the odds are against males bringing up toddlers and preschool children. The situation can conceivably become too stimulating to the man; he either may be unable to do a good job or may find himself engaging in some kind of sexual stimulation with the youngster in his care that will result in discomfort and confusion on the part of the child and a guilty attitude on the part of the male caretaker. In societies where sexuality is a highly charged issue for men—Muslim countries, for example—the use of male child caretakers is particularly hazardous.

In some countries caretakers frequently play openly with the penises of little boys they care for. They laugh over this kind of manipulation and delight in comparing penis sizes among their charges. As one mother recalled, "Our nursemaid would fiddle with our little boy's penis whenever she bathed him or changed him. When I reprimanded her for this, she would giggle, but then go on doing it." Such activities, if they go on regularly, are highly over-stimulating to young children and frequently result in later problems.

Girls may suffer in those cultures that are both extremely Victorian in regard to sexuality and more imbued with the mystique of masculine superiority than is the United States. Hired help in such cultures will favor boys in their charge and belittle girls. The host country nannys will dress boys more carefully and give them a greater choice of foods or more desirable toys unless mothers carefully oversee the development of their children. And caretakers have a whole bagful of stories that can both frighten children and convince them that boys are better than girls.

Another Mother: The Child Caretaker

Departure

Once an adult and children learn to depend on and love a caretaker, there will be no way to depart without some pain and sadness. Yet we all wish to avoid the experience of such feelings. Parents resort to endless subterfuges, denials, and ruses to hide the simple fact from their children that a maid will remain in her country when the rest of the American family leaves for another post.

For example, I was consulted about a five-year-old girl who became morose and lost interest in her parents and in life in general when she returned to the United States. Her mother first became curious about Karen's condition during the long return boat trip to the United States from India, because Karen spent many hours in the seemingly aimless pursuit of opening doors throughout the large ship and could give no explanation for doing so.

Karen had lived most of her life in India under the care of a devoted and playful *aya*. When the family prepared to depart for the United States, Karen's mother could not bring herself to explain that the *aya* would remain in India, her native country. Instead, the family went about their packing and planning for departure, while the *aya* not only left her belongings unpacked but often became tearful or silent. In answer to Karen's questions about the *aya*'s situation, her mother said with some irritation, "She needs to stay here for a while to visit her relatives in Amritsar." Karen then asked, "Will she meet us at the boat?" This question and others were parried with increasing frustration and anger by her mother. Karen gave up asking further questions and fell into the depression for which she and her family sought help.

As the situation unraveled, it became clear the the child, unable to find a plausible explanation for the separation from her *aya*, was tormented by feelings of helplessness, guilt, and anxiety. Such feelings can dominate a young person's life for a long period of time unless separations are anticipated and discussed with candor and warmth.

Suggestions

This chapter has been a catalog of "don'ts," errors, and horror stories because the complicated involvements between members of a family and servants often result in disagreement or overt struggle. Though it would be more pleasant to say that locally hired helpers merely lighten the work of parents and enchant the hours of children, such a statement would simply not be true. The story is a more tangled one. But a family can pattern real and lasting pleasure into its involvements with household personnel by facing inevitable issues directly. Here are some points you might check off when you employ outsiders:

—Make a list of the developmental practices you consider to be healthy for your children at various ages and insist they be followed. Do not let your opinion be changed by an experienced caretaker who tells you, "All children should go to bed with a bottle" (chap. 7).

—Note the qualities you want in a helper and don't compromise. Set yourself the task of training your children's caretaker so that she will be able to carry out your wishes and not her fears and indulgent practices.

—Give the employee reasonable responsibility for your children. Back her up on issues of feeding, discipline, neatness, and respect. Help her to guide your children toward responsibility and autonomy rather than dependence and arrogance.

—Keep some part of your children's daily life as your province. Eat specified meals with them, play with them, read to them, or put them to bed regularly and dependably.

Another Mother: The Child Caretaker

—Learn to be concerned without being snoopy, questioning without becoming undercutting. Set a regular time when your children can talk with you privately about their lives and feelings.

—Do not leave children alone with caretakers for long periods of time and without substantial supervision.

—Talk with your children about departure weeks or months ahead of the event, depending upon their ages. Prepare your stand-in, similarly, in an open way for your departure.

It is never easy to find the perfect "stand-in" mother for a child. The difficulty is compounded by the great differences in certain foreign countries. The moral? Choose well and train even better before you leave a child and native mother alone.

"Overseas you are something special to
your teachers. In the United States you go
back to being just another IBM card."
—A student

IX

A Balance Sheet
on Education

ONE MIGHT SAY that there are two firm anchors in a
child's life: school and home. Of the two, school is the anchor
that can be pulled up more easily and dropped in a new place,
but the new spot must be chosen well and then guarded carefully. The transfer of children to one school or another will
demand an effort that can strike panic in the hearts of unpre-
pared parents, whether the change is from Dallas to Detroit or
from Denver to Dubrovnik. How can the difficulties be
smoothed? Good planning can make a significant contribution. Solid research in advance also helps prevent disappointment later. The whole enterprise can run smoothly if all the
facts are in prior to the move.

Overseas schooling can have its stumbling blocks. "Moving
from country to country and school to school is probably the
worst thing we could do as far as our kids are concerned," one

mother said. "It takes them two or three years to get en-
trenched, find their way, make friends. And then we uproot
them again." Although transience is a painful fact of overseas
living, it is almost as important for families who remain in the
United States and, therefore, certainly is not a reason to reject
international travel. Recognize that schooling overseas will
make geography a natural part of life, language competence a
pleasing accomplishment, and cultural studies a vivid laboratory subject. Most importantly, your children will learn the
main lesson of education: how to get along in the world. A
youngster's province will be the whole world instead of the
narrow confines of a home community.

Let us make a general balance sheet on overseas education
so that you and your family can assess the pros and cons of
your particular situation.

The Positive Side

Overseas education offers wonderfully diverse opportunities to
enrich a child's life. The fascination of acquiring a new language, the uniqueness of a foreign culture, the excitement of
making new and different kinds of friends—all of these induce
families to move overseas in the first place. Overseas schools
are special institutions for fortunate students. The 200,000
American children who attend overseas schools each year typically belong to families who believe in education. The parents
of these young people tend to be the kind who are eager to
enhance the educational experience of their children.

Teachers overseas have chosen the particular countries in
which they work. They are happy to be where they are and
typically show their enthusiasm by their zest in teaching and

the organization of many excursions and involvements in the culture of their adopted country. Field trips to places of great historical interest, happily planned celebrations of international holidays, and sophisticated concern with diverse national cultures are hallmarks of overseas education. Most youngsters overseas encounter educational opportunities far superior to the ones they would have known in the United States.

A headmaster of a school in Italy outlined how his school helped children adapt to the native culture:

> If a child comes in September, when the school opens, the first thing we do is give him a crash course in Italian. We teach him a bit about the city and its marvelous buildings and talk with him about the vocabulary that he has never encountered before. We offer solid lessons in modern mathematics, the regular curriculum, plus the Italian and a great deal in art and art history, so that a child can appreciate being abroad.
>
> The climax of the year is in spring, when we have Renaissance week. Children sing, participate in dramas, recite poetry, and develop mathematics and science exhibitions related to the Renaissance. This experience builds up for two or three months, encompassing the entire school from kindergarten on up, and includes visits to churches, palaces, museums, and other historical places.
>
> The children love their experience here. They often don't want to go home at the end of their parents' tour. In fact, many children call their friends back on the overseas telephone and write longingly about how much they miss being here.

The American overseas community typically uses a school as a major focus for everything it does. The community school in Addis Ababa or Karachi is a gathering place for recreational activities of all kinds. A child's school becomes both a focal point of friendships and a way of life as families move around the world.

The importance of a school for a family overseas may become painfully apparent when children have grown up and left home. As one mother recalled, "I'm just not adjusting as well and quickly to this post because we're alone now. The children made all of our neighborhood contacts, and I kind of got settled into a community through making costumes for the Christmas play and helping with school trips."

The hallmarks of the overseas school can be intimacy and coziness, making it almost the last equivalent of the little red-brick schoolhouse of United States history. Bake sales, PTA activities, and holiday celebrations are shared by the total community. One of the extra benefits for parents is that they know their children's friends. A child, in turn, will have the security that comes from sharing friends with her parents. "I was over at Elizabeth's house," a daughter will say, confident that her mother knows Elizabeth and all the rest of Elizabeth's family. The school for the "dependents" indeed offers a close-knit human experience that seldom can be found in a U.S. metropolis.

Only rarely are parents dissatisfied with the overseas schooling experience of their young. Difficulties may develop, however, if parents complacently move without prior knowledge of the school systems abroad, or without anticipating a child's special needs or considering the lonely child or the slow learner. All these are elements that result in the difficulties that trouble some families.

The overseas school experience is not (and should not be) an exact reproduction of the education a child would receive in the United States. Instead, it should be a unique opportunity to study the world while studying arithmetic, to learn lessons in life as well as lessons in reading. If parents establish objectives for their child's education and keep his particular needs in mind, the youngster will return to the United States saying that he would not have traded an overseas education for the world.

The Negative Side

Some schools are simply inadequate. If your children get caught in one, move them quickly, if possible, or serve generous educational supplements at home. For example, here is how a businessman recalled to me his early schooling in Asia. "It was a very rigid, crowded, old-fashioned school with thirty-five children and a doddering teacher in a small room. It was all very predictable. You were called upon to recite. You stood up, you gabbled, and you sat down. No books, no library, no activities. Anything of that sort was arranged by parents who thought up things that might interest us."

Other distressing situations like the following may arise:

—One child was "harshly thrown into a French school when he had never spoken a word of French or heard French spoken. For three months it was sink or swim and it almost broke his spirit."

—An American couple, as the story was related to me by a colleague, "decided to plunge their children into a Serbian school. The children were speechless for months. All they wanted to do was come to our house and eat peanut butter. Their panic led them to reject everything Serbian. They didn't want to go to the countryside, hear Serbian music, go on picnics, or participate in anything foreign." The physician colleague continued, "Parents ought to think hard before they send their son to a school utterly foreign to anything he has known before."

—"It took me years to find myself educationally when I got back to the United States," said a high-school senior. "Teachers changed constantly. I never learned to think on my own over there, and courses had no resemblance to the ones at home."

These words of parents and children who have been

through the mill may lack objectivity, but they convey an important message. Children deserve to be placed in schools that are appropriate for them. Parents need to pay closer and more consistent attention to the quality of their children's education overseas than in the United States, and to work cooperatively with teachers to bolster weak programs and institute changes where they are needed.

The Schools

Just how do you find the right school overseas, and then decide if it has merit? A number of factors should be studied. First of all, consider the many choices: host country schools, missionary schools, international (American community) schools, Third National schools, Department of Defense schools, boarding schools. A few parents also consider the possibility of their children skipping formal school altogether for a year or so.

In order to anticipate some problems and circumvent others, explore the options open to you and your children overseas. This chapter does not attempt an exhaustive listing (sources of information on schools for overseas children can be found at the end of the chapter), nor does it try to describe schools in detail. Instead, I have culled the views of parents, teachers, and children about the particular atmosphere and psychological setting of certain schools to help parents decide on the appropriateness of one or another.

Host Country Schools

The styles of teaching, learning, and curriculum differ from what children will have known in the United States. American children may well be discouraged by the long hours of the school day, but they will be pleased by what are, to parents, more than adequate vacations. Parents who send their children to host country schools must be willing to accept host country customs in their homes.

Uniforms or a more formal dress code may be required. Teachers may seem unusually strict, and physical discipline may be practiced. Anti-American feelings may run high in certain countries, thus complicating your child's life (and making local schools a poor choice). American children who go to host country schools will, as a matter of course, gain friends primarily among native children instead of American children or other international children.

A teacher in an Italian school put it this way:

> Our Italian children are more restricted usually and very often they go to school in the afternoon. Many schools have two shifts, and the children who go in the afternoon don't get out until after 6:00 p.m. They go to school on Saturday mornings also, which means they just aren't on the same schedule as American children. Italian grade schoolers can't go out and stay for hours at a time without reporting in as American children often do. Italian schools are not set up to deal with the non-Italian speakers, so a sixth grader from the United States may be placed in the first grade, where he starts with the five-year-olds, and, of course, he is miserable. Then, there is still the lock-step discipline. There are no extras and it is all study—no football, no baseball, no art, no music. Some American famiies start by sending their children to Italian schools, but they almost invariably give up about the first of November.

On balance, these schools are suited to young children, unusually adventuresome American children (and their parents), rapid, sophisticated learners, children who already speak the language of the host country, or ones who plan to stay in the same country for many years. Especially on the high-school level, non-American schools can have a profound and lasting positive effect on an American youngster. He will be a citizen of the world forever, tolerant of all nations and races, and particularly interested in languages.

Missionary Schools

These schools typically recruit excellent faculty members who remain a number of years and are devoted to teaching. The courses tend to be highly structured and demanding, which may please many parents but turn off their children. Naturally, a certain amount of religious teaching is part of such schooling, so it is important for parents to learn about the philosophy of a missionary school they want a child to attend.

Most of the students are either host country nationals or the children of longtime missionaries. This results in a certain cliquishness or just a slowness to accept new students who are temporary residents in the country. However, if you recognize that missionary schools were organized to meet specific purposes of a church group, you may find one that will fit your child's needs, for many children have received excellent educations in such schools.

International (American Community) Schools

These are primarily American-sponsored schools financed by a combination of student tuition and American government subsidy. American children form the largest group of students, though a great many international children attend also. The curriculum is similar to that in the United States, and children move freely between these international or community schools and ones in the United States. Most American children fit in without any trouble. They see magazines, posters, and work materials that are familiar to them. The schools are associated with school systems in the United States so that textbooks are familiar and teachers can seek the advice and assistance of colleagues in the United States. In these schools, children remain almost totally in tune with the educational process in our own country.

Since the teachers and principals tend to be on short-term contracts of two or four years, transience may become an important element in a child's educational experience in international schools, and the turnover of teachers may make it difficult for children to develop a true sense of belonging to the school. Children will not know who their teacher will be in the next grade and cannot anticipate having a teacher an older brother or sister especially liked. On the credit side, since most of the teachers are American and have been exposed to education courses that include child development concepts, they tend to be sensitive to special problems and alert to counseling needs of their students.

Family involvement characterizes the atmosphere of these schools. PTA's and bake sales flourish. In fact, because of the yearly turnover, children and parents may have to take a major part in determining the program and character of these schools.

Some parents may decide that international schools are so similar to those in the United States that they repeat a too familiar experience. Yet international schools are certainly the most reliable ones, and short-term overseas families invariably find them to be satisfactory.

Children with learning or emotional problems do best in international schools. American educators are accustomed to such problems and can deal with them sympathetically, whereas some international teachers merely know the need for a stiff upper lip and hard work. Although the work ethic is good up to a point, a major contribution of American educational psychology has been to recognize that motivation, curiosity, and enthusiasm are prime determinants of a child's learning experience.

A Balance Sheet on Education

Schools Run by Other Visiting Nations in a Host Country

Many cities sponsor "European" schools, French *lycées*, German, Dutch, and British schools. Children who want to learn another language would do well to attend one of these. Certainly, the language instruction is intense and ranges from excellent to outstanding. However, a few American children may find themselves enrolled in these schools primarily to play out their parents' fantasies. One girl spoke of being put in a French school in the fifth grade:

> My father decided for some reason that this would be a great time for me to learn how to speak French. So he insisted on sending me to a *lycée*. I hated every minute of it. I had hysterics every morning and I was literally dragged to school and left there. The teachers knew I didn't understand what in the hell was going on, but they didn't try to help me at all, and I really resented it. Some of the students were very nice to me; others simply ignored me or were contemptuous because I was American.

An experienced teacher spoke of further pitfalls that may be found in certain European schools:

> In the European system, the important thing is not so much what you learn but passing the examination. And, of course, the whole idea in the European school system is to weed out as many as can be dropped. In the United States, we think everybody should be educated, but here there isn't enough room for everybody to go to school, and many worthy people are shoved aside simply because they didn't do well on a certain aspect of a certain examination or couldn't deal with the endless memorization and rote learning.

Yet the testimony of many American families is that European schools offer the very best education available in many countries. By American standards, the classes at high-school level are accelerated, with much more material being covered than in the United States. Marginal students, along with those who have low I.Q.'s, are flunked almost automatically, but the particularly able or eager American student flourishes in such a school. The average child may have trouble finding his way.

Schools Run by the Military

The Department of Defense operates a large, reliable, and effective overseas school system for 160,000 American children. Excellent, well-maintained school buildings, good laboratories, and abundant supplies characterize the schools in this system. Because of their centralized operation, these schools are quick to adopt innovations in audiovisual aids, language teaching, or mathematics instruction. Well-paid teachers, often on long-term contracts, impart a stability to both immediate classroom teaching and general educational philosophy. Extensive athletic programs in the larger D.O.D. schools give youngsters an opportunity, often not available in other American overseas schools, to participate in competitive sports. It should be noted that most D.O.D. schools do not place great emphasis on host country studies. However, this concern reaches into the very heart of a family's commitment to participation in the life and culture of the host country. (Chapter 6, "Family Adjustments," and chapter 11, "The Military Family," expand on these issues.)

The dependents of military personnel and other children who can be accommodated in the D.O.D. school system typically receive a uniform, encompassing education that smoothes their lives overseas in a most satisfactory way.

Boarding Schools

Don't overlook these excellent resources for the education of your teenagers. There are many fine boarding schools in Europe and a number throughout Asia and Africa. Though many parents believe boarding schools are geared only to the pocketbooks and views of wealthy expatriate families, this is a myth held over from another era. Because of the great number of internationally mobile children from many countries, these schools attract a cross section of highly educationally motivated children. For the most part, overseas boarding schools are staffed by well-trained teachers who, because of small class size, can individualize learning opportunities and offer activities to satisfy the interests of a wide range of students.

To prepare for such an experience, parents must be sure that their teenagers are ready to leave home and be on their own. Before going to boarding school, a teenager should have learned to take care of his clothes and room, to handle money effectively, to fend for himself in new situations, and to have a considerable knowledge, however blunt this advice may seem, of sex, drugs, drinking, and risk-taking behavior (concerns discussed in chap. 10, "Adolescents").

Boarding schools are a hallowed part of the tradition of overseas life for good reasons. They have proved themselves to be exceedingly valuable resources for the education, maturation, and general broadening of generations of children.

Boarding schools in the United States offer another important alternative for families to consider. Because it is convenient to learn about them directly when you are in the United States, we will not consider them further.

Other Options

No Formal Schooling

Have you thought of simply offering your children independent study for a year? I am sure they would welcome the idea, and it is really no great hardship for parents. Many families have chosen this alternative and found that their young blossomed marvelously under a regime of reading, correspondence courses, self-directed learning, travel, and simple indulgence. A year in which to lie fallow can give a youngster a healthy new perspective on education and, at the same time, allow him to develop his own pursuits and find a renewed closeness with his parents. On the other hand, there are certain shortcomings as well. A young person may lose study habits and soon be completely out of step with other children. A sense of discipline may be lost, along with a feeling of responsibility.

Correspondence Schools

These schools can be used either as a supplement to learning or as a prime educational tool. Historically, they are among the oldest types of American schooling abroad, and many effective adults are products of this special system of education. The parents who become teachers in this system must be prepared to sort out the complicated roles of teacher, facilitator, disciplinarian, nurturer, and friend they assume when they don these several hats. If at all possible, try to get several families together for such an arrangement so that a child's mother does not become his only teacher, for this tends to muddy the relationship between mother and child. Correspondence schools demand a high sense of motivation and strong self-discipline from a young person.

Separating the Family

Teenagers often dread the prospect of moving overseas. A sixteen-year-old girl may balk at going to Arabia with her parents when she is in line to become a cheerleader; a sixteen-year-old boy may complain about being forced to trade the opportunity to play football in a fast league in order to move to a Latin American city where friendly soccer is the only sport. Although boarding school should be considered for these teenagers, many who don't go to boarding school but wish to remain in the United States can make totally satisfactory arrangements for themselves by living with relatives or friends while they complete high school.

Parents often overestimate their children's curiosity and appetite for seeing Renaissance paintings, ancient ruins, and crusader forts. Some children totally conditioned by life in the United States simply will not thrive without McDonald's hamburgers and American-style bowling alleys. For children who are rooted in their own home town traditions, it is worth considerable effort to find a local residence where they can continue their high school years comfortably. Naturally, the U.S. military outposts also offer an American environment.

Some Practical Suggestions

Talk with school officials at home before you leave and ask what will be expected of your children when they return two or three years later. Find out what courses will be covered and get a copy of the syllabus for those years. Keep in touch with your local school officials to be sure that your child is keeping up adequately.

Parents who fully participate in the culture of the country in which they live will find that their children can be quite comfortable in host country schools or schools run for English, French, or German children. These schools can be an exceedingly fine experience for children, though the dividing line is usually the second grade. After that, the curriculum diverges and it becomes difficult for a child to catch up when he returns to an American school system.

Parents must participate more closely in the education of

their children overseas than they do at home. It is wise to visit the school about once a month and sit in on classes, thus finding out how you can help if there are weaknesses in the school. Some parents actually become immersed in curriculum planning and arranging for holiday events, trips, dances, and athletic events.

Learn all you can about your new post's educational opportunities before you go and discuss these with your children. Plan to check on the correspondence schools listed here and utilize courses from them that can enrich your child's experience. It is wise to apply early for entrance to the selected school and to take along the student's credentials. Be sure to get copies of grades and course descriptions from the overseas school. These documents will be helpful when you return to the United States.

If you do use a host country's school, try to have your children placed with others their own age. It is often a great temptation to place children who do not speak a foreign language with a younger class, in which case there are no age mates to play with and difficulties develop. Language tutoring can be a more satisfactory answer to helping a child catch up with his peers.

It is sensible to talk with one's children about the pros and cons of moving overseas for their schooling, sound out their particular worries, and help them to discuss them. A child appreciates having a parent say, "I know you're disappointed that we are leaving Washington just when you have gotten on the basketball team. It's tough to give up things that you care about." Such an opening can allow a child to pour out his unhappiness and then begin to make a new stab at understanding his total family's needs as well as his part in planning for a move.

A *Balance Sheet on Education*

Educational Planning Aids

Calvert School, Tuscany Road, Baltimore, Maryland 21210.

Correspondence Instruction, Extension Division, University of Nebraska, Lincoln, Nebraska 68503.

Department of Defense Overseas Dependents Schools, Department of Defense, Washington, D.C. 20301.

High School Correspondence Courses, University of California Extension, Department of Correspondence Instruction, Berkeley, California 94720.

Maher, A., ed. *Schools Abroad of Interest to Americans*, Porter Sargent, 11 Beacon Street, Boston, Massachusetts 02108. 1975.

Office of Overseas Schools, Department of State, Washington, D.C. 20520.

Science Research Associates, Inc., 259 East Erie Street, Chicago, Illinois 60611.

Also consult your local teacher's college or university school of education for information about enrichment and correspondence courses.

"I had a lot of emotional problems just
because I couldn't do what was natural
when I was sixteen."
—An adolescent overseas

Adolescents

MANY PARENTS will agree with this view of a
mother in Africa who told me: "A real advantage of living
here is that our daughters are removed not only from television
but also from many other undesirable elements in their environment back home. The drug problem is almost nonexistent;
we have far fewer fights about dating and none about the car."
On the other hand, adolescents themselves tell a different
story, especially as they look back at their experiences in retro-
spect at a time when they are struggling to find a place in the
mainstream of American life. "When I visited the States two
years ago, it really scared me," a seventeen-year-old I interviewed in Asia told me. "Seeing Americans dig ditches and
wait on tables in a restaurant was strange," he continued.
"Over here you walk down the street and everyone looks at
you. You're on stage all of the time. Back there you miss all
the attention. You become an unperson, yet you feel odd
because teenagers in the United States are more sophisticated
in clothes and contemporary thinking and everything."

Adolescents

Unfortunately, the advantages of being an overseas adolescent may turn out to be short-lived. Adolescence will run its course, and children cannot always be protected. Young people need to move out on their own, choose their own interests, make their own friends, and learn to govern themselves. Too many parents may ignore the teenage years of their children, only to find that the typical adolescent turbulence was not avoided but only postponed until their teenagers eventually returned to the United States. For every adolescent problem put off there is still an impressive catalog of dilemmas for families to face when they move overseas. Happily, workable solutions can be achieved through initiative and understanding within families and support from the community.

Certain adolescent issues are universal, at least for American teenagers, and need to be kept in mind before one considers the special conditions of life abroad!

Adolescents are painfully aware of their bodies and tediously preoccupied with clothes. Their adherence to fashion is almost cultlike. Growth is rapid and physical changes are conspicuous.

Pulling away from parents and turning to their peers for guidance is normal. Adolescents need to test themselves, make mistakes, and, ultimately, to settle on a way of life. They crave the freedom to prowl around in strange parts of town, to waste or use time, to daydream about jobs and activities chosen by themselves.

Sexuality and romance preoccupy them. They need privacy to sort out these emotions that will later determine their adult happiness as partners and parents.

It is hard to imagine many situations that are less conducive to facing and working out these issues than an overseas post, where the following conditions typically exist:

Clothing Styles

A fifteen-year-old American may wear two-tone shoes to a new school only to find that local young people prefer shiny black shoes. American blue jeans, though highly prized worldwide, are not accepted attire in some capital cities of Asia and Europe where youth may favor stylish dresses, well-cut jackets, and ties. Americans are bound to feel as awkward and out of place as an adult would in the same circumstances.

Hang-outs

The hamburger stands, bowling alleys, movie theaters, and 3.2 beer places that cover the United States don't exist in most other countries. The movie *American Graffiti* could never have been filmed in Africa, for instance, where adolescents are unable to get driver's licenses and therefore can't cruise in automobiles. So the teenager must depend, for his recreational needs, upon the very family his instincts tell him he ought to be drawing away from.

High Profile

American teenagers are highly visible in a foreign culture; they are a part of our "presence." At a time in their lives when they feel clumsy and uncertain, the continuous concern with manners, length of hair, and style of dress may well drain spontaneity and even some of the charming roguishness from an adolescent. One mother of two teenagers put it succinctly:

> I think our State Department should tell ambassadors to lay off teenagers. They shouldn't be tied in with their parents' official behavior. A father's efficiency rating should not depend on the way his child dresses. For a kid to be clobbered with the role of the Ugly American and the fear that he may hurt his father's job if he

doesn't cut his hair is disastrous. It's too much at that age to carry the United States on his back.

She went on to say, "If the ambassador said to me, 'Cut your son's hair,' I would answer, 'It's none of your business.'" What a brave mother!

Dating and Sexuality

Teenagers who move to certain countries abroad often feel as though they had been suddenly whisked away by a time machine to a small town in nineteenth-century America. Everyone knows what they are doing, or can find out about it, and the range of acceptable behavior may be limited by the views of the most narrow-minded members of the community. Here are some of the situations that surface overseas:

A sixteen-year-old girl became involved with a man from the embassy of a country whose relations with the United States were somewhat strained. Many members of the American community volunteered their opinions about the propriety of the friendship.

A fifteen-year-old boy solved his sexual problems by frequenting one of the many brothels in Bangkok, where he lived at the time. His parents learned of this and were horrified.

A sixteen-year-old girl who had lived in Africa with her parents most of her life dated host country schoolmates as a natural event. After the family returned to the United States, the girl brought a black boyfriend home from college. Her parents were disturbed.

Work

The time-hallowed practice in the United States that a teenager, regardless of his economic status, will find a job, perhaps as a gas station attendant, a shoe salesman, or a janitor, is definitely not a reality of overseas living. There is little opportunity for youths to work overseas, and you hear such comments as this one from a sixteen-year-old girl:

> I couldn't work because girls just don't go out of their houses in a Muslim country. My brother couldn't work either because there wasn't anything for him to do. I mean, there just simply wasn't anything. So we spent our summers at the club swimming pool. I had highs and lows about it. Basically, I think I had a lot of emotional problems just because I couldn't do what was natural when I was sixteen.

Schools

An adolescent expects high school to combine a variety of extracurricular athletic, social, and artistic events. Overseas schools do not offer the range of activities available in most American high schools. Sports, drama, music, painting, sculpture, school government, clubs, and the like are often unavailable in the overseas school environment.

What Is Left Behind?

The adolescent who moves overseas must leave behind his familiar props—the record collections, television programs, teachers who think well of him, stores where he is known, shady neighborhoods, and hidden places to ride bicycles and perhaps share a cigarette or an exciting erotic book. He also leaves his close friends, the ones who assure him that he is okay, that his family is impossible, and that growing up is worth a try.

Teenagers who have difficulty making new friends in the United States may find their problems compounded in far-flung countries. Some fortunate youngsters land on their feet anywhere on the globe and feel at home immediately. But for many, the period of transition is painful because youthful social circles are notoriously excluding. Adolescents who get "in" are so relieved that they can't be bothered with the "outs." An American teenager in Saudi Arabia described what it was like where he lived this way:

> When kids first get here, they're in shock. Life is so different from what they've been used to—the physical layout of the school and the whole thing about their families getting settled. There is a kind of hostility and competition. It's caused by fear—of not being able to speak the language or being able to get along with the other kids. Most of them just wander around in a daze the first month. After school, they go back to their own houses, which are quite a distance from each other. If they do make friends at school, they sometimes have their friends come over. But that doesn't take care of it all.

Ironically, new arrivals often gain acceptance first from the "out group" teenagers in a school, the fringe youngsters who are least comfortable in the setting. Another teenager tells of this experience in a new school overseas:

> Everybody sat there and looked at me and at what I was wearing. You get to the point where you'll be friends with anybody who's friendly to you. One of the guys that was friendly to me wasn't my kind of person. He was into drugs and bad-mouthed everything about the school. But I was lucky because later I got to be friends with some other people.

These are trying problems, among the most challenging ones that teenagers and their parents face in their new environments. What can be done about them? The following ideas and suggestions, are some that have worked for many families and communities.

The Art of Anticipation

Learn all you can about a new post before you go—the location and size of the school, the availability of a kiln for potters, competition for a football player, clubs for sociable youngsters. Teenagers deserve to know the true reasons for making the move. Be honest with yourself and them. Allow them, and yourself, a mini nervous breakdown. Then pull yourselves together and pack the clothes, records, posters, stuffed animals, stamp collections, tape players, and books you will need.

Families

Parents and children will probably spend more time together than they ever dreamed of sharing in the United States. Don't allow the pleasing camaraderie that develops around meals, museum visits, travel, or picnics to obscure your teenagers' natural needs to show independence and even some rebellion.

Teenagers need freedom to be on their own. It makes little sense to demand that they be perpetual representatives of the United States of America. A parent who agreed with me about the concept of independence in general nevertheless closed our discussion with this admonition: "When my boy lives here in Washington, he's just Robert; but when he goes to Latin America, he'll be the son of the Deputy Chief of Mission and in the spotlight." My advice to parents is to keep the spotlight as dim as possible.

Teenagers need a lot of leeway so that they can gain experience in making choices in their lives. On the other hand, parents retain ultimate responsibility for their children's behavior; this means a willingness to intervene when necessary. The basic standards set at home are the best guarantee that a child will make responsible decisions for himself. A parent's trust in him will bridge transient periods when his language, dress, and manners don't exactly conform to one's highest ideals. Fortunately, most school administrators are concerned about the same problems and welcome parental cooperation in the development and maintenance of healthy student rela-

sons, mostly organized by the fathers, particularly of the middle school, where they had about thirty fathers and sons playing football. This year, they played soccer. The kids really like soccer, but it's tough on the fathers—just too exhausting for them. We have a school bazaar and cake sale, a big dance around Christmas time, and some teachers organized hiking and skiing trips.

One of the consequences of a narrower range of outside activities is that the adolescent has more time to study. This should be recognized by all concerned as an opportunity to gain a great deal of educational strength. Parents can help considerably by monitoring their teens' work with thoughtful involvement.

Work

Work opportunities in the American community should be explored and even manufactured. Aptitudes and motivations are uncovered through actual job experiences. Consider carpentry, painting, child care, and volunteer work in hospitals. Perhaps, as a last resort, students could be paid for doing their school work well. Admittedly, jobs for teenagers are scarce in communities where human labor is so inexpensive, and the natives may take a dim view of such use of our teenagers. But for a teenager, a job solves two problems for him and his family—he has something to do with his free time and such work cuts down the amount of aimless or disruptive activity that teenagers lapse into when they don't believe they are valued by society. If at all possible, teenagers should be paid for their work, for there is no adequate substitute for money as a criterion of worth in today's adult world.

A *Helping Hand*

When an embassy official or oil company executive genuinely welcomes new families, including their children, and extends a helping hand to them, that attitude will diffuse through the entire community. Since a point of view tends to filter from the top down, adolescents will know whether or not they are genuinely wanted by deeds—a welcoming visit from a government official, an introduction by the school principal, or a party for teenagers given by parents in the community.

A big brother or sister could be assigned to each new student to talk with him about how people dress, where they congregate, and what they enjoy doing together. Big brothers or sisters should not only function in the first week but should also make periodic contact with recent arrivals for a number of months to check on their adjustment.

Adolescents profit from involvements with adults outside their parents' group of friends. Communities might identify formal or informal counselors to work with adolescents. Coaches, ministers, or members of volunteer organizations can be most helpful listeners and guides. In the United States, teenagers often will seek out on their own someone away from their family to rap with, and it is important that such a possibility be made available overseas.

Clubs

Every post with a considerable American population should have a club where teenagers can listen to records, drink Cokes, and play games. Group activities such as meditation, play reading, or shared hobbies develop naturally in favorable settings. A teen club should offer privacy and space.

Return to the United States

For many young persons, the real hurdle is not finding a way to fit in overseas but trying to "make it" when they face the traumas of transition back to the United States. Although some youngsters return to their original school and resume old friendships and activities, others sweat and strain as they try to find a place among their American peers.

One teenager related:

> I felt out of everything when I came back. I didn't know about music or clothes. I was still listening to Motown when everyone else had become more sophisticated. I expected everything in the United States to be in terrible shape, since that was the way they made it sound in the newspapers and *Newsweek*.

Another told me:

> I lived in Egypt and India before I came back to go to a large high school here. I was miserable the first few months, and my parents never knew what I was going through. I was over-developed physically, but I never really realized it until I got into school here. That and boys expecting you to go to bed with them right away were just too much for me. It made me feel so odd. I just wasn't aware of it ahead of time, that people really do go through these kinds of problems.

An adolescent overseas might wish to keep in touch with the United States in order to know what records are popular, the kind of clothes that are being worn, and the names of sports stars and actors. Perhaps copies of *Rolling Stone* and other magazines could be made available and records and tapes received on a regular basis. Parents overseas may feel secretly relieved that their children are not in the mainstream of American culture. But their children often feel lost when they return to the U.S. and don't know what is "far-out," what is "cool," what is "for real," and what is "heavy." (See chapter 14 for more on these issues.)

These may seem to be superficial concerns to an adult burdened with international trade agreements, wars, and famine, but they are by no means unimportant to adolescents. Attention paid to them will greatly facilitate the transition a foreigner has to struggle with as he makes his way in a new land. For, after all, the United States is a foreign country to teenagers who have been away for a long time, and they need all the help they can get when they try to make sense of it.

XI

The Military Family

The Military World

It would hardly be fair to equate the lifestyles, outlooks, and day-to-day activities of civilian American communities overseas with the unique characteristics of the military enclave. Military life, whether it is on base or off base, for the high-ranking officer or the NCO, forms its own protocol and molds the behavior of everyone involved in it. When a man dons a uniform, he learns that he must live according to a special code, and he passes along his views and concerns to his wife and children. This chapter will focus on those special aspects of living that must be considered by the largest group of Americans now living overseas. Similar treatments might well be given to the corporate executive and his family, the missionary group, or the "oil men." Those in such specific fields might check on what is unique about their own group's style of life as we treat the challenges for armed services families.

The military man's life is more programmed than that of his

civilian counterpart, and psychiatric surveys show that his children tend to be better disciplined than those of non-armed forces families at home. According to a study done by Dr. James A. Kenny, a child psychologist at the Wiesbaden Air Force Base, the incidence of delinquency for military children ages ten to seventeen was only one-fourth that of the U.S. average.* Dr. Kenny summarized his views of a military family's life in this way:

> First, the father with his "command and obey" military background is more apt to be strict. *Obedience* is a military virtue; self-expression is not. The father may translate the military manner into the discipline of the children. A second factor which lessens acting out among children is the total authoritarian impact of the military community. The father is in a duty status twenty-four hours a day, seven days a week. He is responsible for the behavior of his dependents. For example, if a child misbehaves on the school bus, and the father does not take appropriate corrective action, the case may be reported to the father's commanding officer.

Dr. Kenny, a former Air Force officer in Germany, also points out that "everyone knows everyone else" in the Army post. This makes for a close-knit situation much like that of the U.S. rural community, where delinquency is also low. At the same time, of course, in contrast to the civilian in his Frankfurt villa, privacy decreases for the military. Husband, wife, and children lead a fishbowl existence.

The military world overseas is a special world. To the man, financial rewards, which can add up handsomely with allowances and benefits, often count for less than duty, honor, and country. The Army, in return, "takes care of its own," and a tour of duty—as a natural part of a career—has great enticements. At the same time, the military professional (and his family) do not always take advantage of all the possibilities.

* J. A. Kenny, "The Child in the Military Community," *J. of the American Academy of Child Psychiatry,* 6:51–63, 1967.

Some American families, particularly those of enlisted men, will be shy about venturing outside their compounds. The "good life" is inside the American military colony. Although the Special Services offer intriguing trips, many families prefer the post movie house. Some wives prefer to shop at the PX, where everything is familiar, rather than the colorful markets of Europe or Asia.

The trip overseas naturally begins at home, and experts advise that families pose certain questions and seek answers before departure time.

Preparation

These are among the questions that preoccupy military families as they plan to move overseas:

"Will I be able to buy children's clothing in Germany?"

"Should I keep my charge accounts?"

"What about cooking ingredients and utensils?"

"Shall I take small appliances, such as hair dryers and toasters, or not?"

Check with Army Community Services and Air Force Family Services for answers to many questions, and, if the system of sponsors is working in your area, write to people already at your future post to help with others. The system of "sponsors"—families designated to help entering personnel find their way at a strange post—can be a godsend to bewildered neophytes. It is wise to write the sponsor long in advance of departure to inquire about voltage used and the need for transformers. The military family already on location can answer questions about post washing facilities and the usefulness of bringing one's own washing machine.

A few letters between the American family in Washington, D.C., for instance, and a helpful family with the U.S. Army in Mainz, Germany, can ease housing and driving problems.

The Military Family

The sponsor can supply a list of available rentals near your post or procure a booklet on driving regulations from the local automobile licensing agency that you can study before your arrival. "A good sponsor makes all the difference," says an Air Force major. "He sent us a Rules of the Road book when we were still in the States. Then I was able to get licensed soon after we got to Germany. Once we had wheels under us, life took a turn for the better."

The First Days

Some people feel lost at the start. A sergeant recalls his initiation to Germany in this way: "When you get there and can't even read a road sign, use a telephone booth, or count money, everything seems bleak. My experience is that you reach the bottom in about three months. You think you are at the end of your rope, but then somehow you start coping and things begin to get better."

Special problems arise for those who must live "on the economy" or in isolated villages away from the military post. A young Army wife shared the following recollections with me:

> You have no one to talk to. You are dependent for everything. When you can't get to a PX, a washateria, or a market on your own, you feel like a little child. The situation breeds a lot of frustrated women who then decide they didn't want to come in the first place and, because of their shared frustration, don't even try to use facilities that are available to them.

Prescriptions for Settling in Happily

One mother solves the problem in this way: "Within a day or two of getting anywhere, I set up house. I take our pictures, bric-a-brac, dishes, bedding, and books and set them all out right away. I try to make the transition as quick and painless as possible. I don't worry about perfection, but just get it done."

Once in a new place, women can seek out opportunities to use shuttle buses to get around for shopping and washing. Group expeditions organized by military wives can help to decrease the sense of isolation and helplessness that is so often felt. When necessary services are not available, families can band together to find such services for themselves. Children's play areas, for example, can be discovered or created by families working together. Women can combine baby-sitting and household tasks. One mother might learn about the local transportation and introduce new families to it.

Most wives agree that "getting involved in the culture makes all the difference." When overseas Americans begin to learn the language of a country, use local markets, and explore the local sights, all the problems—housing, school adjustment, and shopping scarcities—lose their importance. This is a critical point, for, as one woman told me, "Many people just won't leave their houses. They say, 'It's dirty out there and too different.' But if you're frightened of being overseas, then you don't get into the culture. You fall back on yourself and all the other lonely people who reinforce each other's depressions."

Solutions

Sponsors at a new post might develop booklets and newsletters that describe local conditions. Briefings about schools, recreational facilities, and ways to get into the culture prove very useful. Post letters help to orient newly arrived families.

Of course, the happiness of children is paramount. It can be insured by the availability of recreation halls, teen centers, gyms, soccer and baseball fields, ping-pong tables, and swimming pools. Activity programs of all kinds are as essential as opportunities for trips to interesting parts of a new country. Do such opportunities exist at the post? If they don't, a family can band together with other families to develop some programs. Isolation can be combatted by pulling together to do the washing, shopping, and chauffeuring of children. "When you find people who are excited about where they live and curious about going to see things, the excitement becomes infectious," advised a major's wife. The provision of regular trips through community service bureaus can fill a great void when a family is new to a country and not yet ready to venture out into the culture on its own.

Discussion groups with qualified leaders help ease the overseas American into a host country culture. Because suspicions arise if activities are made "official," it is important to organize social and recreational activities outside of command channels and with the participation of the people who will use them.

The concepts of anticipation and preparation should be integrated into a family's day-to-day thinking. Then, though one looks to the Army to "take care of its own" in emergencies, a person will be free of chronic dependency during ordinary times. Of course, the planning, future-oriented stance can become an irritant. A lieutenant in a preparation group voiced such a complaint:

> I'm getting depressed by all this talk about troubles, and I don't want to hear anymore. I felt going to Berlin would be great, and now you've gotten me to worrying. When I bought a house in Virginia, I bought it because we liked it. Then I found out about all its troubles. I feel the same way about going to Berlin. I don't want to know that it has leaky pipes and lukewarm water; I just want to go to Berlin.

The above complaint seems natural enough. But this stance can breed difficulties, for, as the saying goes, "The problem of the ostrich with its head in the sand is not only that it won't see anything but that it may get kicked in the behind."

Living Arrangements

Along with love, work, and sustenance, human beings also require adequate shelter. In many instances—perhaps in most nowadays—military families receive suitable quarters. Exceptions occur, of course, when for one reason or another the U.S. government fails in its duty and the housing is either inadequate or not affordable. A disgruntled sergeant puts it this way: "If a landlord rips you off, it means that the assignment and the country turn sour." The situation is particularly critical for civilians attached to the Army.

Housing worries become a lightning rod for many other discontents, perhaps because military families—in contrast to other Americans posted overseas, whose housing is secured by their companies or the U.S. government—frequently must make their own living arrangements based "on the economy." This unique part of overseas military life needs constant attention from everyone concerned. What are the most common problems? A family may have to live in barrack-style dwellings whose impersonality grates on the nerves. Houses may be too small or apartments too cramped, especially for a family with children. Because of local conditions and a scarcity of housing, the members of a family may have to occupy separate quarters.

Here are some other problems as told to me by military men or their wives:

"Some landlords are worse than the apartments they rent. You come into an apartment and find wires sticking out of the wall. You have to put up your own light fixtures. You often have to share a bath with the landlord. Sometimes you don't have hot water heaters. Refrigerators are tiny and the washing machines boil your clothes rather than clean them."

"The 'stairwell' apartment houses are breeding grounds for everything bad—dirt, noise, unhappy and uncontrollable children."

"Many families in my area could not get concurrent travel paid and, because military housing was always filled, separations of three to six months occurred regularly. Families moved when it was convenient for the Army, not for them, and children often had to change schools in the middle of a term, unless a wife delayed her arrival and therefore increased the length of separation."

"Economic difficulties sometimes have pushed families off their posts into separate quarters," says one long-time military father. "Inadequate civilian housing, much less attractive than families had known in the United States, and marked isolation of the families from both the European community and the Army community compound their problems. As an escape from these depressing circumstances, wives may exaggerate the need to return to the U.S. to 'take care of my sick mother' or drift into an unhappy stay overseas."

Because of the economic burden and the unpredictability of housing overseas, many wives actually decide to return to their own parents' home with children while a husband serves an overseas tour. Though such an arrangement offers considerable support, women who choose it find that they have been relegated to a childlike role once again, subject to their own mothers' and fathers' wishes. Children become confused when they don't know who is in charge of a household; it is difficult for them to understand how their own mother can be treated like a child.

Solutions to the Housing Problem

All experienced hands agree that husbands should make special efforts to precede their families and negotiate housing on their own. A man on his own can size up the housing situation more quickly (and plow through waiting lists more effectively) than a father who feels the pressure to get a roof over his children's heads that very night. Certainly the government should be encouraged to provide adequate, affordable living arrangements as the highest priority for making new families comfortable.

Fathers

Overseas life can be trying. One father complained:

> You can't relax, it's a pressured 24-hour-a-day job. When you are over here and there is something to be done, you have to do it, because there are so few people available. You are on the scene; you live on the post. So they call you. We're always understaffed; there is always tension and you never feel you have completed a job. Your family suffers because of this, and you just count your days until you can get back to the United States. It gets to my wife and children when I just can't be with them, especially when they had become accustomed to my coming home at night, getting out the barbecue grill, and spending the evening with them back in the States.

When a father disappears on military maneuvers or other distant assignments, family structure alters radically. The mother loses a crucial part of her support system and must take on a new authority role. This often results in considerable growth on the part of a woman, but it may complicate her relationship with her husband. One mother put it this way:

> Many women get a big charge from being overseas because they are forced to become independent when their husbands are away. They change from being the "little wife" and find that they become effective, independent human beings. Husbands have to watch out, though, because when they do come home they may find that their wives took over many of the jobs and prerogatives in the home."

The place a woman can carve out for herself overseas depends, as one father put it, "very much on the personal security a man can count on in his own manhood."

If the father remains the center of the household, the mother needs to create a satisfactory role for herself. One wife analyzed the situation as follows:

You find a great deal of over-mothering because the only place women are really needed is with their children. So wives overcompensate when husbands are gone by requiring their kids to stay home a lot more. They overfeed them and overprotect them. A son may be put in a husband's role, and all kinds of troubles develop.

Another mother offered these intelligent comments about the problem of the absent father:

A lot of women develop crisis personalities in the Army. The only time we really feel good is when we are handling a crisis. So we *make* crises. There is nothing else to do. We are definitely not needed in the military, but we often are not needed by our husbands either. It's a paternalistic society in which the Army takes care of the men but forgets the women. Men attach themselves to a company commander or first sergeant and fulfill their lives through work and dedication. It can be very gratifying for them, but nothing is left for their wives or children.

An Army obstetrician-gynecologist summarized the end point of such a situation: "I see sixty-four women a day. Their husbands have been in the field for two months. Their bank accounts are overdrawn, their kids are in trouble at school, and their periods are three weeks overdue."

This physician has several solutions. He advised that

Men and women in the service need to learn how to sort options, make priorities, and decide what is really important in their lives. Wives should talk together about their mutual needs so that they don't look outside of their families either to alcohol or affairs for gratification. Husbands and wives must find ways to be closer when they are together and to develop meaningful activities for themselves and their children.

The Service Itself

Many military people develop valuable insights about their peculiar lifestyle. "Giving and obeying orders are so much a part of overseas life, and rank is so built into the military situation, that many fathers never think to have discussions with their children at home," a military wife recalls. "Fathers think teenagers will follow their lead, but their children are not in the Army with them. A thirteen-year-old girl is not going to worry about the Army's mission when she wants to smoke pot."

Another woman added:

> Fathers try to run their homes like they do their companies. Some men never take off their uniforms even when they are at home! They give demerits and chew out their children in foul, parade-ground language. Let's say a sergeant has had a hard day. He comes home, looks at the duty roster, and finds that his teenage son has not taken out the garbage in three days. He calls the kid before him for inspection, reads him the riot act, and then tells him he will do his work or get so many demerits. Then the punishment he gives out is unbelievably disproportionate to the crime.

Even concerned fathers may overlook the needs of their families. "We were in Europe and things went well for us," a colonel recalled to me, "so I told my family that we would extend our tour; we'd stay until July. My children refused. They just refused! At first I couldn't believe it. But then I had to agree that they counted too."

The colonel spoke with wisdom. He recognized that the lives of all family members, including the children, of course, are equally important. Unfortunately, military men don't always embrace this viewpoint for their families because they have become accustomed to a different outlook. In a professional soldier's judgment, the operative principle is command rather than discussion. (For more on this see chapter 6.)

What Can Be Done?

To be sure, military families must adapt to military requirements and accept the reality that fathers will be away for long periods of time. By the same token, the entire family should decide if a wife and children will accompany a father overseas. Although the unaccompanied tour may be practical for the man, it can be disastrous for his children. Left without a father for long periods of time, they are put under unusual stress and often suffer from the lack of a needed role model at crucial moments in their lives.

It is not easy for a man who has built his life around military authority to leave both career and iron discipline at the front door when he comes home. He must try, however, for families thrive on discussion more than orders, involvement rather than heroism. And a change of pace can be refreshing for all concerned.

Fathers who must be away a great deal might make special attempts to be with their families in a scheduled fashion when they are home. They could plan, for instance, to work with clubs to which their children belong. For example, a definite schedule can be set in which a father and son go swimming together. Another time, daughter and father could play tennis or take a walk together. And a husband must set aside a definite period each week to be alone with his wife. Unless he makes a time investment, the marriage will hardly prosper in the often difficult overseas climate.

Children

Although educational opportunities overseas are of a generally high quality, recreational activities often leave much to be desired. Yet these opportunities need to be sought out. Says one officer: "We joined a German tennis club and our son played on a German soccer team. We met all sorts of people, and it was great. When you do something together with them, the Germans are great."

It is true that the transient nature of military life creates built-in problems. "Our children never finish anything. They start on model-making and then we get orders to go to a place where you can't buy models. Our daughter began ballet lessons, and we moved to a post where there was no interest in dancing," a former overseas mother recalls. When children must move a great deal, parents might direct them toward individual activities such as music, stamp collecting, or rock and mineral studies. A child should choose his own hobby but will need support and encouragement to continue it. Parents can help, especially at times of flagging interest on a youngster's part, by keeping a ready supply of needed materials at hand.

Parents can also help compensate for inadequate educational resources. "I flooded my daughter with books when we were in a place where the school was just mediocre," a mother recalled. "I tried to provide her with lots of cultural experiences to make up for what she was missing in plain school work. I believe that the chance to go to operas, to talk to people, and to ride on their trams and trains makes for education of a rare kind."

There is also the often present dilemma of boarding schools. Most American families would not ordinarily consider sending a child to one. However, because of the small number of teenagers on many posts, it has been necessary to set up centrally located boarding schools for dependents. The special section in the chapter on education covers many details, including preparations to be made.

A military family might also consider the many civilian boarding schools throughout Europe, as well as several that exist in the rest of the world. Most are democratically run and welcome children from all racial and national backgrounds. Tuition fees are not oppressively high and subsidies often are available. The reputation for "exclusiveness" is based on a few such schools in England and Switzerland and, with some isolated exceptions, no longer holds true today. The Army

The Military Family

Community Services Branch, the Air Force Family Service Bureau, or the counselor in your youngster's school will be glad to steer you toward the best choice. It is most helpful to visit a number of these schools, and, despite the cost, an orientation trip generally proves worthwhile.

Some teenagers will do best to stay with relatives and attend high school back in the United States in order to remain in the American culture during the crucial adolescent years. Chapter 1 describes the basis for such a decision.

Foreign-Born Wives and Mothers

How about cross-cultural marriages? The latter can add a strain to military life overseas. For example, a German wife always has her own parents, as well as other relatives, around her. She is in touch with her brothers, sisters, and grandparents by telephone. She will see her family frequently if they live in the same city. Children of these marriages grow up to be different from other Americans. The mother's parents back up the German societal values of orderliness, achievement, and quietness. The American father, meanwhile, may feel left out and even resentful. He may push his young son into Little League while the German mother and grandmother will be saying, "Learn, learn."

Difficulties are almost inevitable when a foreign-born wife is torn away from her folks and her milieu in order to move to the United States.

Adjustments can be made with genuine success only if the parents anticipate problems that will arise and reach agreements among themselves about standards of behavior they expect from their children.

Final Words of Advice from Families Who Have Been Through It All

—"Dig in your heels if you are asked to move in the middle of the school year."

—"Send those who want to go, prepare them for going, and then pay attention to them when they are overseas."

—"Unaccompanied overseas tours are never uncomplicated. They are either the cause or the symptom of family difficulties."

—"It is not so much whether to go with your family or not but how the family decides that makes the difference in the success of an overseas tour. You always have to ask if your wife and children had a chance to make their input into the decision."

In summing up, one might say that the military family is actually lucky. Adventure beckons. There are no severe financial problems. Everything is paid for and generally taken care of. Dismissal and a sudden termination of income are rare. Economic security prevails. And those problems that do exist will yield if attention is paid to family priorities as well as to military requirements, housing arrangements as well as job specifications.

XII

Children's Fears and Worries

IN ADDITION to the catalog of creatures who frighten children in the United States—goblins, monsters, grotesque TV characters—older cultures, which have had far more time to develop a genealogy of ghosts and spirits, can supply even more troublesome figures to keep youngsters awake at night and scare them in the daytime. The following are some samples:

—"My *aya* in Afghanistan taught me that the *Deaiu*, a giant who captures human beings and then feasts on them, lives in the mountains at the end of the world. She also convinced me that when you stumble in the dark, you have tripped over a tiny creature called a *jinn*."

—"In Italy we had a maid from the coast who would tell us that if we didn't eat, *Babo Natale* would take us away. We never knew whether to believe her or not. But it scared us."

—"An old man called the *Bodie Mala* lived in a field near our house. When I did something my *aya* didn't want me to do, she would take me over to the field and hand me to him. That's all I can remember about it except that this man was really terrible looking. It's funny, but I never told my mother about him."

—An American teenager who grew up in Germany said, "I spent my entire childhood dreading the nightly story from the gloomy *Ring of the Nibelungs*. I think the key to German monstrosities is there and not in Prussian militarism."

—"I remember when I was young in India the hyenas howled outside the house at night. They made scary sounds, and when I was bad my *aya* said the hyenas would jump through the window and snatch me up."

A young child is particularly susceptible to such strange ideas and frightening creatures. From two years of age, when logical thinking and imagination develop, until approximately five, when a child has achieved some control over his thoughts and can differentiate somewhat between fantastic fears and realistic concerns, his head may be filled with all kinds of disturbing thoughts. Though his life situation may well exaggerate these anxieties, it isn't unusual for a healthy two-year-old to wake up at night screaming in terror and remain frightened the next day.

Developmental Stages and Fears

(Kidnapping) Most children go through a stage in which they fear that they will be stolen or carried away. These fears of kidnapping preoccupy three-year-olds and then recur again at adolescence. When such terrors coincide with realistic worries about political kidnappings, parents and children alike are burdened with demanding concerns. Kidnapping has always been a prime fear of children, and that fear is heightened now by the publicity given to the kidnapping of Americans in foreign countries. Your help to place this fear in perspective will ease anxieties for the whole family.

Emphasize the unlikelihood of kidnapping. In those few areas in which kidnapping is a realistic danger, familiarize your children with the security guards who protect the community of Americans. Establish definite boundaries for play and travel areas; make a schedule for telephone check-in times; provide adequate adult supervision for leisure activities. Offer a home environment that minimizes the development of fearfulness in your children.

The expected hurdles of child development form a background to fears, which occur more frequently when children and parents struggle over toilet training, feeding, or other issues involving independence and control. Children who are told grotesque fairy tales or who are kept on too tight a rein by their parents will become particularly fearful.

Each developmental stage has its problems of too little and too much. If a five-year-old is given too much freedom, he may become frightened by his own impulses. If he is held in too tightly, he becomes afraid of showing any kind of aggression. The latter tends to be turned inward and will show itself in the form of fears and phobias. Therefore, a parent should first consider how the adult and the child handle developmental stages when they attempt to solve particular fears (chap. 7).

Prevention

Understanding is important when it comes to prevention of these childhood terrors. Understanding begins with the knowledge that worries about separation and loss are at the base of most childhood fears. Because they are so dependent upon adults, children are vulnerable to anxiety when they feel that they may be abandoned or that they are unloved. Stability and reliability on the parents' part are paramount. Children need to know when their parents will be home and when they will return if they are away. Any separations can bring out questions, uncertainties, and even irritation. Parents should, therefore, insure that young children live in stable environments where they are cared for by loving people who give them understandable rules to follow. In the same sense, children deserve reliable caretakers who radiate security and dependability. If parents must be away from home for any length of time, a child should be prepared for that separation and, as described in chapter 8, a caretaker in whom parents have total confidence should take over for them.

Some fears, while not appearing rational to the adult, may be accepted as normal. But fears or phobias that interfere with a child's ordinary activities justify the seeking of psychiatric help, for they may be expressions of deeper problems that need to be worked out.

A child should be encouraged to approach new activities positively. When he first goes to school or leaves home to play with other children, when he first sleeps alone or tries a new skill, he should be given a run-through of the activity with assurances and appreciation from his parents. He needs to hear a father say, "I know you'll have a good time at your friend's house," not, "I'll come over and pick you up early if you have any trouble at your friend's house." All children need opportunities to increase their autonomy, and, in fact, all childhood development should be seen as an opportunity for a child to become more independent and self-reliant. When parents themselves see separations as healthy challenges, they will communicate that comforting point of view to their children.

Bedtime

Many fears begin at bedtime. They can be circumvented by preparing your child happily for bed with a story, a quiet game, or even a pleasant talk after he is tucked in for the night. The child should then be allowed to go to sleep in his own quiet room, possibly with a cherished toy under the sheets with him. This is particularly important to children of families who are traveling or must move frequently from one post to another. The toy or security blanket or other familiar object is soothing because it represents some constancy in the child's life. Children also get great comfort from the rituals of bedtime. If these rituals are honored all the time, children can take all kinds of uprooting without anxiety.

If a child wakes at night, he should be comforted and pleasantly put back to sleep. There is no place for harshness at such times, though children will greatly appreciate definiteness and firmness on the part of their parents. If a child wakes up at night and comes downstairs, he should be taken back to his room and put to bed with reassuring but explicit statements. He will then learn that his bed is a safe place. A child may ask to sleep with his parents when he is frightened. This should be discouraged, since the child then will not be able to master his anxiety about sleeping alone. The parent should also ask himself the crucial question: Am I transmitting my own fears to my child?

Parental Attitudes

Children fear their parents' disapproval more than anything else in their lives. Parents who habitually scold children or are harsh in their anger encourage a timidity and hesitancy on the part of the children that often is transformed into fears of fantastic animals and monsters. Gentleness and consideration are needed. Lean down to speak with a child, use his words when speaking, and be certain not to be overly repressive in what you say. In the heat of anger, a parent might think of unusual punishments that he would never carry out. The most painful punishment for a child *is the threat of loss of love.* If a parent says, "I'm going to give you away if you do that again," or, "I wish we could send you back to the United States," the child is literally helpless. Guard against such statements and, if they do slip out in anger, be sure to discuss them with your child so that they are seen as products of a moment of trouble and unhappiness and not your true feelings.

Children need to be reassured that they are lovable to both their parents. Though children of four to six years of age will choose sides between their mothers and fathers, parents need to remain evenhanded in giving love to their daughters and sons. When a girl sits on her father's lap and kisses him passionately, her father might accept these manifestations of love with warmth while still telling his daughter how much he likes her mother. A mother whose six-year-old son is devoted to her and critical of his father needs to help her son recognize that she doesn't buy all of his complaints about his dad. This is a time when parents need to be united themselves and also to be sensitive to their children's developing needs so that no room is left for the encouragement of fears.

Parents need to examine their own attitudes toward fears. They should not joke about their own fears with children. A mother who says, "I'm afraid of cockroaches and Johnny is just like me," will confirm her son's incipient fear. Children are extremely sensitive to a parent's concerns about darkness, lightning, thunder, or deserted houses. What is needed is for parents to figure out their own problems, either among themselves or with the help of a doctor, so that they can master their irrational concerns and thus strengthen and comfort their children.

Be careful not to transfer your disappointment in a country to the lizards, kidnappers, or dirt that may or may not exist in that country. Children can understand and deal with straight talk about difficult jobs or boredom; they can't deal effectively

with issues that are veiled in vague concerns about the am-
bience of a country. A parent must get his own house in order
or, at the very least, not share the disorder of that house with
his children.

Household Help

Household helpers present particular problems in regard to
the inculcation of fears. One must constantly be on the lookout for any superstitions or worries related by caretakers to
children. These predictable fears include loss of life, kidnapping, being eaten, tortured, or transformed, sexual concerns,
and the dangers of animals. It is well to discuss this list of concerns with both children and baby-sitters so that the children
can separate the real dangers of a particular society from the
imaginary ones. Even though this strategy can't eradicate all
the problems, it will help a child master many concerns and
place others in a realistic perspective.

Sex

Concerns about sexuality often seize children when they
become aware of their bodies. These preoccupations can be
turned by a small child's mind into a fear that the child will be
punished in some awful way for a wish to play with his penis or
her vagina. Children worry about the differences in their bodies. A girl may conclude that she lost her penis because she
was bad; a boy may worry that he might lose his penis because
of his bad thoughts. Obviously, these concerns can be dealt
with when parents themselves are comfortable in talking directly about sexuality and when they can explain body differences as naturally anatomical. A single statement tells it all.
"Boys are made one way and girls another; one isn't better than
the other." This statement needs to be elaborated and dis-

cussed in detail, but it captures all the existing facts. Parents need to take time to deal with the sexual concerns of their children and be ready to answer repetitive questions that children will ask about sexual differences.

Guidance

It is far easier to prevent fears by attending to the developmental issues from which they spring than it is to treat fullblown ones. Sometimes, however, a child will be seized by an intense fear or phobia without any apparent stimulus for it. A three-year-old, who is particularly vulnerable to fears, might recoil at the sight of a snake or a swarm of insects. Then, out of their own uncertainty, his father might force the child to touch snakes or his mother might scour the house to free it of all insects. Both acts only intensify a child's fear.

If a fear develops, tell your child that you recognize his anxiety. Allow him to talk with you about his worries and reassure him about the innocuousness of the object or the rarity of any genuinely dangerous contact with it. If he develops a fear of snakes, you might encourage him to draw pictures of snakes; take him to the zoo to visit some snakes; buy him a rubber snake to handle. If a parent is comfortable with snakes, a child will borrow some of that comfort and, in many cases, gradually lose his fear. Praise your child and perhaps even give him a reward as he becomes more comfortable in dealing with snakes. This technique is the basis of positive reinforcement therapy, a most effective method for treating patients who have specific fears.

If you are unable to help your child by rational, gentle discussion and involvements with the object that has aroused the fear, at least reassure him that he is not "bad" for having such a fear. Continue to treat him as you do your other children, but recognize the seriousness of his concern and seek help for the problem. Parents can get help from other parents, a doctor in the community, or a psychiatrist, if available. A psychiatrist can find out, for instance, if the fears are exaggerated and actually signal deeper problems in a child.

Many such problems are developmental in nature and gradually wear away over a period of months if they are not reinforced or exaggerated by poor handling on the part of parents or servants. A child who has a specific fear should be assured that the object of his fear will not overtly harm him. He should know that you recognize how painful the problem is for him. At the same time, urge him to adhere to his usual activities, such as sleeping in his own bed, going to school, or visiting with friends. Chapter 13 deals with serious problems that cannot be resolved by the measures just described.

"The one thing I wish I had done before I
left the United States was to take a First
Aid course."

—A mother in Turkey

When You Need Help:
Medical and Personal

MOST PEOPLE, particularly those whose previous
travel experience has consisted of visits through the capital cities of Europe, may worry about shots but little else of a medical nature before embarking on an extended overseas tour.
However, settling down in one place for several years differs
greatly from hotel hopping, and the excellent medical facilities
you can depend upon in London may not be matched in the
Middle East. Though common sense and hope may go a long
way toward keeping you and your family healthy, it is advis-
able to carry a medical and psychological "First Aid course"
mentally with you throughout a tour overseas. You simply
have to take more personal responsibility for your well-being
overseas than you would in the United States. The ideas that
follow are meant to give you, and your family physician, some

knowledge of how to prepare for a move and what to do if trouble erupts.

Preparations

Long before you leave the United States, take the time to get each member of your family a thorough medical examination. Check off all the problems and questions you can think of: a teenager's acne, a father's hernia, eye trouble no one had bothered to see a doctor about before. Ask your physician to give you a copy of his records, including immunizations and a supply of growth charts for children, to take with you. Blood pressure readings, blood counts and other laboratory reports, and a general statement of a person's physical status can be extremely helpful to a new physician when he sees a patient for the first time.

It is no longer necessary to have a valid smallpox vaccination certificate in order to enter or leave the United States and many other countries. However, certain countries still require valid smallpox, cholera, or yellow fever certificates. A useful pamphlet called "Immunization Information for International Travelers" can be ordered from the Superintendent of Documents, Government Printing Office, Washington, D.C. It will give you all the information you need, though your own organization can undoubtedly fill in details and the Medical Division of the U.S. Department of State, Washington, D.C. 20520, is happy to send information on various countries. Your city health department or State Department of Public Health can provide you with immediate phone information about immunizations needed for international travel, and can also administer shots at a low cost.

Many people live with minor disorders that bother them only occasionally. Such disorders may be overlooked in the rush of moving. Some disturbances to note before you leave the country are migraine headaches, allergies, recurrent eye infections, a tendency to stomach upset, asthma, skin disorders, anemia, weight problems, arthritic difficulties. When you attend to these problems, talk with your doctor about what to anticipate in the treatment of them over a long period of time. If any member of your family has diabetes, thyroid disease, or epilepsy, be certain that you understand the medications used and ask your doctor to give you some idea of potential changes in treatment that might be called for in the future. Ask him to anticipate any emergency care that conceivably might be needed.

Take an ample supply of all the medications needed for long-term illnesses in your family. Though almost every country in the world stocks adequate supplies of medicines, it may be a while before you can make contact with a pharmacy that can fill your prescriptions accurately. Many people who must take complex or special medications have found that it serves their needs best to order medicine from one of a number of pharmacies in the United States that make a specialty of expediting shipments of medicine overseas. Addresses of reputable pharmacies can be gotten by leafing through the advertising pages of the *Foreign Service Journal*. When a particular medication has been ordered, get the exact one prescribed and not merely a similar preparation that may be available in the country where you live.

Check on all dental needs before departure. Braces and other orthodontal concerns must be decided on so that you don't have an unhappy teenager with crooked teeth on your hands when you are far from reliable orthodontal care.

Carry prescriptions and extra pairs of glasses from your ophthalmologist. Ask your optician if he will speed a new pair of glasses to you if you need them. Check on the possibility of continuing to use contact lenses in your new post.

Your family physician can get information about special medical needs in various parts of the world. Anti-malaria medication is indicated for some places, salt tablets for others. Some physicians recommend a shot of gamma globulin to guard against infections when settling into certain countries.

Preventive Medicine

The Growing Child

American children are among the tallest and healthiest in the world. Studies of general body growth and illness profiles show them to be at the very top of the health scale. Though the exact basis for these findings is not known, it is reasonably clear from research studies that several factors are of prime importance. These include: regular maternal and child health checkups; the use of nutritious foods and vitamins; and the alertness of American pediatricians to the ordinary developmental problems of children. American physicians typically diagnose and treat developmental problems of children— growth retardations, nutritional deficiencies, eye problems— and, by doing so, prevent complications.

American pediatricians have pioneered the concept of health maintenance and preventive pediatrics based on a schedule of regular checkups on a child's growth and a great deal of research on normal physical and emotional development. These concepts are new to other countries where doctors frequently are inundated with acute, emergency illnesses that take up all their time. It is only when doctors have the lux-

161

ury of doing research on development and seeing well patients that they can work at the concept of health maintenance. The concept is an extremely important one, for much of the general health and vigor of American children can be attributed to the fine health maintenance care offered by American pediatricians. Obviously, the same concepts hold for the care and treatment of adult health needs.

Suppose you can't find a physician sophisticated in American health care techniques? First, consult a book on child development to familiarize yourself with what to expect at each stage in a child's life (chap. 7). Keep your own child development records, utilizing the physical and emotional growth chart forms you got from your physician in the United States. You will find it interesting to follow the changes in height and weight, the steps in motor coordination, and the characteristics of psychological development in each of your children. Then, if you notice any significant deviations in a child's development, you might wish to seek a developmentally trained pediatrician or make contact with your home town pediatrician.

If your family's pediatrician recommends regular examinations for your children, ask your local pediatrician to schedule regular visits if he does not suggest them. All pediatricians can do examinations of bone and dental growth, vision and hearing, and cardiac status even though such examinations may not be a regular part of office routine, just as regular adult health examinations are not considered necessary even in the United States at this time. However, a somewhat higher index of concern for growing children overseas will pay off in healthier children.

Food Habits

Get specific dietary recommendations for babies and growing children from your family physician. Stick with the feeding schedule you have learned and don't permit infants and young children to be fed according to local fads or customs at variance with your own. Consult a book on nutrition in order to become familiar with the components of a healthful diet. Left to themselves, host country caretakers will fill children with the staples of their regions: pasta in Italy, cous-cous in North Africa, rice in South Asia. Each of these foods can be the basis of a healthful diet if rounded out with other protein-rich and vitamin-filled foods; when used as the whole diet of a child or adult, nutritional deficiencies may occur.

The use of protein supplements may be necessary in some countries, and regular vitamin intake may be helpful. In regions that do not have fluoride in the drinking water, children should use a fluoride-fortified toothpaste and fluoride tablets (Cari-tab, Fluoritab, etc.) or fluoride-fortified vitamins (Vi-Daylin with fluoride, etc.) to prevent cavities.

Long-Term Needs

When a child has had rheumatic fever or a fracture, many doctors overseas—as well as in the United States—will consider their work done after the acute problem has been remedied. Doctors may not think of prophylactic or rehabilitative measures, yet these very measures prevent complications and insure healthy growth.

For example, children who have had rheumatic fever should be given antibiotics throughout their growing period as prophylaxis against streptococcal infections. A careful exercise program helps to restore full function to a limb after a complicated fracture. Prompt mobilizations of patients after operations speeds recovery and reduces complications.

Yet physicians trained in an older tradition may order patients to remain in bed for long periods following an appendectomy. A child forced to languish in bed may gain weight out of boredom, refuse to take up his usual activities when he leaves the hospital, and feel that he has become an invalid for life. A good surgeon and supportive parents can encourage a child to participate in activities reasonably and progressively. On the other hand, the timidity of both surgeon and parents may conspire to encourage a child to favor a limb that has been fractured, or refuse to play contact sports long after an appendectomy.

Although you must get individual advice from your physician, the best general advice is to remember that children are amazingly hearty and resilient. After a reasonable period of time (the definition of a "reasonable period" must be determined by a physician who knows your particular child), children should be allowed to participate in all of their usual activities if at all possible.

Unusual Theories, Unusual Treatments

—"Our two-year-old had a pleasantly protruding belly button, but our first pediatrician was horrified by this and insisted on taping a coin to the child's umbilicus. When our caretaker changed the bandage and put a silver good luck coin on the belly button, the doctor was absolutely furious and said it had to be a copper one. Todd went around with a dinar glued to his tummy for weeks."

—"Children should never eat cold foods in the winter because they cause pneumonia."

—Some overseas doctors treat lower bowel upsets by stuffing patients with mashed potatoes.

—Intramuscular injections for almost any problem—obesity, sexual difficulties, failure of growth, undescended testicles, fatigue—are favorite treatment methods. Some of the hormones used are extremely powerful and can result in major disturbances in body metabolism. In addition, the hazard of contracting hepatitis or other infections from the needles used in intramuscular injections is always present. The best solution is to protect your children from shots if at all possible or to ask your physician if he might use single-use plastic syringes and needles for treating your children. Some parents stock a supply of single-use needles and syringes to be available for emergencies that might arise.

All peculiar theories and treatments should be sifted through your own good judgment and the wisdom of any experts available to you. A great deal of what passes for medical treatment is innocuous, but some therapeutic ideas can be overtly harmful. Therefore, in some cases you just may have to second-guess the opinions of doctors.

Handicaps

Some physicians temporize when they should treat children with certain handicaps. If a child has an undescended testicle, a spinal curvature, or a foot disorder, the overseas doctor may tell parents to wait until they return to the United States to have the problem checked. Subtle cases of physical growth deviation may be neglected because many doctors just do not have the training or skill to deal with them. Therefore, seek a doctor who knows about such problems and assure yourself that you have gotten an accurate evaluation. If you are still dissatisfied, consult your home town pediatrician by phone.

Cleanliness

Many habits that merely reflect good manners in the United States or Western Europe make eminently practical good sense in countries where intestinal parasites carried by water, feces, or direct contact are endemic. Stringent standards of cleanliness can be put in force if the reasons behind them are explained clearly. Children, and even adults, will accept and practice careful habits of good hygiene if they are given adequate preparation and observe consistent models of disease-preventing cleanliness before they leave the United States.

165

Children can be taught to wash their hands each time they use the toilet and to keep their hands and fingers out of their mouths and eyes. Some habits may be reinforced by making a game of them. Washing hands might be rewarded regularly by stars, and children might be encouraged to count the mosquitoes or flies they swat as if an insect war were being waged. A child with a tumb-sucking or nail-biting habit might consult a pediatrician or child psychiatrist before leaving the United States to correct the problem.

Food

Be certain that all members of the family wash their hands before eating. Warn children never to take food from floors or local markets. Dissuade them from accepting food from strangers.

Since children learn best by the example set for them, be careful how you deal with food and cleanliness issues. The parent who tells his child to wash his hands before eating but doesn't do so himself, or admonishes a child who picks up a pastry from a fly-covered mound of sweets but then takes one himself at a later time, only confuses the child and thwarts the promotion of good habits.

These warnings will be unimportant in those countries that have standards of hygiene equal to or better than those in the United States. However, even if you are going to a highly developed country, but plan to stop off on the way in a tropical area, be sure to observe scrupulous rules of hygiene.

Your Kitchen and Food Handling

A neat kitchen will help prevent stomach upsets. Always keep a kitchen spotless. Wash dishes immediately after use. Don't leave food out where flies can get to them. Refrigerate everything you can.

If you have a cook, teach her the food handling rules of your house and watch her like a hawk for at least a month. Tell her why you are particularly concerned with cleanliness. Repeat the steps you feel are necessary to insure cleanliness. Some cooks must be taught to wash their hands after a trip to the toilet, to use boiling water, to wash dishes, and to put food away in a refrigerator.

You may be embarrassed to be a snooping overseer, but it will be useful, for, as one woman recalled, "In Tunisia many cooks consider a table clean if they have swept away the flies, even though a one-inch crust of dirt and debris remains." In the Middle East cooks typically use water from the *jube*, or ditch, to wash vegetables. Such a practice adds insult to injury, for both the vegetables being cleaned and the water in which they are washed may contain the very same parasites.

Your snooping must go even further in many cases, for some cooks, not surprisingly, will say one thing and do another. A cook may state that she boils drinking water twenty minutes, washes her hands before she prepares foods, and peels all vegetables carefully, but actually do none of them when you don't watch her. The head of the household must become a kind of hygiene tyrant in countries where disease is an important issue.

Be certain that all food handlers in your house are healthy. Medical examination when you are concerned about illnesses and feces examination if you live a country that has endemic intestinal parasites provide useful health insurance. Discourage the relatives of your servants from hanging around your kitchen.

Good Hygiene

These simple principles should be taught to every food handler in a household. Because misunderstanding about these hygienic principles often develops, let us review them briefly:

Microscopic bacteria can be found everywhere in a house. All of us carry millions of bacteria or germs, most of which are not causes of illness, in our mouths, intestinal tracts, lungs, and on our skin. In addition, germs and parasites are carried by insects and animals.

In most highly developed countries, germs that cause such diseases as malaria and typhoid fever have been eliminated through medical attention to water and sewage and eradication of insect carriers. In countries that lack adequate sewage disposal, treated water systems, and other safeguards of public health, germs that cause disease migrate through direct contact, feces, and the water and sewage disposal systems.

Therefore, in order to keep healthy in countries that have important infectious and parasitic disease problems:

—Do not use unboiled water. It doesn't matter whether water looks fresh and pure or dark and muddy. What does matter is the number and kinds of bacteria in it. Boil water for twenty minutes to kill disease-causing germs in it. Carbonated beverages may not be safe if the bottles used have not been sterilized. Ice cubes may not be safe. Freezing does not kill most germs, and the water in the cubes may be contaminated.

—Do not eat fresh fruits and vegetables unless they have been boiled. Since feces may carry parasites and manure is often used for fertilizing crops, disease-bearing germs may be present on fruits or vegetables. The best rule of thumb is, "If you can't peel it or boil it, don't eat it."

—Always wash hands after defecation to prevent transmission of parasites from a bowel movement to the rest of the body. Encourage everyone in your family to keep their hands out of their mouths and eyes, since germs from their bodies or other sources can be introduced into the body in these ways.

—Be sure your milk supply is non-contaminated or boil all milk used.

—Do not eat pastries covered with whipped cream if refrigeration is not adequate, for warm cream is a lush breeding ground for certain disease-causing bacteria.

—Avoid dogs, bats, and skunks, for they may carry rabies. Obviously, get immediate treatment if bitten.

—Screen against mosquitoes, which may carry malaria, and flies, which typically frequent manure piles and carry diseases from the manure. One only slightly fanciful old-timer's prescription for eliminating flies from a bedroom was to place a bucket of manure (non-disease-bearing) on a porch nearby. The flies would swarm to the manure and leave the rest of the house free.

Disease precautions are most relevant to tropical countries that, because of lags in development, have not yet conquered many public health problems. However, transient stomach upsets may incapacitate a traveler anywhere. The medical basis for such upsets, which occur even in the most highly developed countries and to travelers who are scrupulously careful about food and water, is not clear. However, physicians who have studied the problem attribute it to differences in the microscopic content of tap water from country to country and, in some cases, to the bacteria *E. coli*. Many travelers believe they will evade stomach upsets by drinking only bottled water as they move from country to country.

After some months in a country, residents frequently dip into the tempting specialities in pastry shops or venture into well-recommended local restaurants. Little trouble ensues, for a mysterious accommodation characteristically takes place between local foods and American constitutions. In any case, when that accommodation is not perfect, stomachs are quick to complain.

Don't frighten yourself unduly about the dangers of exotic foods, for occasional fevers and stomach upsets are associated with overseas living, just as fleas accompany dogs. And, fortunately, most diseases can be treated effectively. You may defend yourself against diseases by choosing to live in a sterile environment, but you would then miss much of the pleasure of life overseas. If you practice sensible health habits, get regular medical and laboratory examinations, and report to your doctor any symptoms you develop, you can live healthily overseas.

The Choice of a Doctor

When you see your family physician for the last time, ask him to recommend a doctor at your new post. Many physicians know medical school classmates or professional colleagues to whom they can refer you with confidence. Ask friends who have lived in your adopted country about the medical care available and the names of specific doctors. When you get to your new country, ask people in your organization and the American community about reliable doctors and, certainly, check with the local American embassy or consulate, since embassy officials maintain a list of reputable physicians. Keep in mind, however, that the embassy cannot make value judgments about physicians and that it will be important for you to talk with your friends in order to find the kind of doctor you want.

Competent physicians can be found everywhere in the world. Even in less developed countries and, certainly, in the capitals of Europe and Asia, there are numerous doctors who have had fine training in excellent medical centers. I have worked with impressively capable physicians in new countries of Africa who display diplomas from respected American hospitals or European universities.

When You Need Help: Medical and Personal

It does take effort to find these well-trained doctors, just as it does in the United States. Because the physicians you encounter overseas will have come from a great variety of schools and backgrounds, choose among them thoughtfully. By skillful inquiry among friends and physicians, you can discover which "school" of medicine—American, French, English, or German—dominates the country in which you live. Then if someone in your family has an illness such as diabetes or obesity, for which there are a variety of treatment preferences, you can choose a physician whose background fits the treatment plan you have chosen with your doctor in the United States.

Doctors overseas typically concern themselves with the treatment of acute rather than long-term illnesses and overlook problems in child-rearing. They often focus on immediate care rather than the problems of rehabilitation that may take a long time to resolve. They may over-treat children who have fevers or infectious diseases. Some show a kind of zealousness in their use of antibiotics and a tendency to prescribe massive doses of medication for disorders that might resolve with mild supportive treatment or none at all. Many physicians overseas are quick to give shots and pills, and a lot of both, when time might be the best treatment. Of course, similar situations can occur in the United States, but you might be on the lookout for such practices whether you live in the United States or overseas.

Physicians, like everyone else, have personalities, and you will want to choose a doctor who gives you a feeling of comfort and confidence. You might even choose one physician to treat acute illnesses and another to deal with developmental and personal problems.

Once you have chosen a physician, depend upon him and assume that he knows what he is doing. However, if someone in your family develops a serious illness that leaves you puzzled or anxious, keep in mind that it is possible to ask for a consultation from another physician or to travel to a medical center for consultation. This is a touchy subject, for some doctors seem to consider it an insult if a consultation is requested. However, if you find yourself concerned about the medical progress of someone in your family who has a serious illness or for whom a decision about radical treatment or surgery needs to be made, request a consultation from another physician. When a person's entire future is at stake, tact should be sacrificed to accuracy.

Hospitals

If your family is in tip-top health and you don't anticipate any concerns, there is no great need to check on hospitals in your city. However, if one of you—a pregnant wife, a child with diabetes or asthma, or a husband with significant high blood pressure—might need hospitalization at some time, be sure you know where to go. Learn about hospital admission procedures and treatment facilities. Then, in case of any emergency, you can be admitted to a hospital with a minimum of anxiety on your part. Before the need for hospitalization develops, identify someone who speaks the language of the host country and can be available to interpret effectively your medical needs to the personnel of the hospital.

When You Need Help: Medical and Personal

When Illness Strikes

Home Treatment

A certain amount of fever and diarrhea invades any household. Children will develop mumps, ear infections, chicken pox, and the flu just because they are children. Many parents have learned to diagnose and care for the common infections and cuts and bruises of childhood. It isn't necessary to call on a doctor for every stomach upset that hits your house if you can become competent at recognizing when to intervene, when to let nature take its course, and when to call for help. As one woman recalled, "The one thing I wish I had done before I left the United States was to take a First Aid course."

Any experience you can get in a hospital emergency room, pediatric ward, or medical clinic will be helpful to you when you are on your own and need to make decisions about an illness. The books on medical care listed at the end of this chapter are well written and can supplement your knowledge and abet your common sense when you have forgotten the incubation period of scarlet fever or you become flustered at caring for a child with a high fever.

See Your Doctor

Whenever you feel out of your depth in looking after a sick member of your family, a visit to your doctor is in order. Don't delay out of anxiety, but become comfortable in making regular visits, particularly if you live in an area where illness is an expected accompaniment to life.

All parents are anxious when their children become sick. This natural anxiety may show itself in various ways. Some parents will become over-solicitous, others irritable and ineffective. Still others might withdraw from care of the child or other children in their family. Whenever a child becomes sick, Mother and Father must pull together and be sure that they agree on handling the illness. The child in bed needs to be kept interested in life so that he doesn't become more interested in remaining sick.

The job of caring for a sick child is often left on the shoulders of a mother, but a father can be most helpful when a youngster is sick and in bed. A regular stint of reading, playing games, or changing bandages can help both the sick child and a tired mother. A father's work overseas may seem to make it difficult for him to spend time with a sick child, but ambassadors and generals have carved out time to be with their ill children. One executive simply left his desk and stayed by a son's bedside for three weeks until a particularly stubborn fever passed.

Hospital Treatment

If a child must be hospitalized, stay with him at the time of admission and, if at all possible, bring along someone who speaks the local language. Visit regularly, no matter how many tears well up when visiting hours are over.

Try to stay in the hospital with a young child. The separation for hospitalization often is the first time a little child will have left his home. American hospitals, aware of the trauma of such a separation, have liberalized visiting hours and made provisions for mothers to stay with their sick children. European hospitals, and others throughout the world, have adopted these innovations slowly and with some reluctance. Perhaps you can work to increase the pace of change in such care practices in your local hospital.

During a child's hospitalization, considerable planning may be required to maintain his ties with home. Bring him favorite toys and books and tell him what is happening in the lives of sisters and brothers. Even if the hospital is a rigid one that does not permit visits by children, carry the sick child to a window so that he can see his siblings.

Keep a sick child abreast of progress in his treatment and describe the rationale and steps involved in procedures that must be performed on him. If he does not speak the language of the doctors and nurses, he will benefit from the help of a regularly available intrepreter.

If you are not satisfied with the diagnosis and treatment your child receives, take him to the capital city for a consultation with a highly trained specialist. Telephone service is now so good worldwide that many parents simply call their trusted doctors at home to get advice on a difficult illness. When you are uncertain about a treatment being used, it can be extremely helpful to have the support of a doctor who has known you or your child for many years.

These hints apply just as much in the care of sick adults, whose needs sometimes are disregarded in an overseas situation.

A Travelers' Medicine Cabinet

The following descriptions of common disorders and medications for them was developed in conjunction with physician colleagues overseas. They deal with most of the ordinary problems that crop up. I have included both popular brand names of medications for purposes of identification and also the generic or chemical names, since these can be identified throughout the world, even if a particular brand name is not available in a country where you live. Consult with your physician before treating yourself, except in times of great emergency. I have included specific instructions for treatment in case of just such emergencies, or if you feel the need to check on the treatment plan of your physician. Be sure to get prescriptions from your own doctor, who can instruct you about dosages and side effects as well as allergic reactions that may occur to susceptible individuals.

Before going overseas, ask your family doctor to give you some emergency medicines to control pain and deal with minor colds and infections you may contract, until you have a chance to locate a doctor where you will live. If you are taking medicine regularly, be sure that your doctor gives you extra prescriptions, using the generic or chemical names of the medications so that they can be filled easily when you get to your new post.

Every household should keep a supply of these basics: Band-Aids, one-inch gauze squares, and adhesive tape. Phisohex (hexachlorophene) liquid soap for cleaning cuts and skin infections. Thermometers. Neosporin Ophthalmic Solution for minor eye inflammations and infections. Calamine Lotion for skin irritations from prickly heat, poison ivy, sunburn, or insect bites. Dusting powder, such as Johnson & Johnson Baby Powder, for skin and foot irritations. Throat lozenges or cough drops. Suntan lotion. Aspirin or Tylenol (acetaminophen) for minor pains of all kinds. Narcotic pain relievers such as codeine should not be stocked because of the dangers of over-medication and, in rare cases, addiction. Carry an ample supply of aspirin and avoid over-the-counter pain relievers sold worldwide, for some have been shown to produce serious blood disorders.

Diarrhea

Mild stomach upsets pass with the use of a bland or liquid diet. Ginger-ale and other carbonated beverages help many people. For prolonged diarrheas not attributable to serious inflammations of the gut, such as appendicitis, or to parasitic infections, Lomotil (diphenoxylate hydrochloride with atropine sulfate) has become widely used. Most other medications have been superseded by Lomotil, which also helps to decrease vomiting. The use of Lomotil may mask underlying infections, so be certain that it is used under the guidance of a doctor. If fever or abdominal pain persist more than several days, or blood appears in stools, get immediate medical consultation.

Itching

Itching from persistent skin infections, insect bites, and severe sunburn can be controlled by a remarkable medication called Temaril (trimeprazine).

Colds and Other Upper Respiratory Infections

Ornade (ispropamide, chlorpheniramine maleate, and phenylpropanolamine hydrochloride) or other drying agents are most effective in stopping runny noses and the associated symptoms of a cold. Benzadrex (prophylhexadrine and menthol) or other inhalers make breathing easier and are particularly useful for the relief of the discomfort that results from change of altitude during air travel.

Toothaches

Gargle with a warm saline solution, then apply Eugenol, a topical anesthetic, directly on the tooth.

Motion Sickness

Bonine (meclizine hydrochloride) or Marezine (cyclizine) quiet upset stomachs, though these medications make some people sleepy. Anti-anxiety agents such as Valium (diazepam) may be useful to relieve severe tension related to flying.

Fungal Infections such as Athlete's Foot

Minor infections are best treated with good hygiene (baths, dusting powder). More serious ones respond to griseofulvin (Fulvicin, Grifulvin), Tinactin, or Desenex. However, any serious skin infection should be examined by a doctor before treatment is started.

Allergies

Antihistamines such as Benadryl (diphenydramine hydrochloride) offer effective treatment. Benadryl and several other antihistamines are also useful sedatives.

General Infections

All general bodily infections require consultation with a physician. In a great emergency, when no doctor is available, penicillin preparations, such as Ampicillin, or broad spectrum antibiotics, such as the tetracyclines (Declomycin, Sumycin), might be considered for use. However, the danger of hypersensitivity reactions, particularly to penicillins, must be kept in mind. No person with a history of hypersensitivity should medicate himself. Any emergency self-medication should be followed by a visit to the doctor, since accurate treatment of infections is critical for good recovery.

Minor Cuts and Skin Infections

Clean thoroughly with Phisohex or other disinfectant soap and cover, if necessary, with any of a number of anti-bacterial ointments, such as Neosporin or Bacitracin.

Burns

Apply ice immediately to limit the tissue damage of any significant burn. Wash burns and keep them clean; expose them to air if at all possible in order to promote healing. If a burn is likely to become dirty because of exposure, cover it with a dressing, but change the dressing daily. If redness and pus develop in a burn, the burn is probably infected and should be treated by a doctor.

Psychoactive Medications
(Tranquillizers, Anti-Anxiety Agents, Sedatives)

Since so many people in the United States use these medications—about 30 percent of adults take psychoactive drugs and they account for 25 percent of all prescriptions—they may form an important component of the medicine cabinet for some families who plan to live overseas. Obviously, it would be best to diagnose and complete treatment of anxiety and sleep disorders before you leave the United States so that the use of psychoactive medications will not be necessary overseas. However, for those who, under the advice of the physician, must continue to take these medications, the following list describes when their use is generally indicated. Many of the medications have disturbing side effects and none should be used without the advice of a physician. The effects of all these drugs can be increased by alcohol consumption. The use of any of them carries with it the risk of adverse reactions, habituation, or addiction. Generic or chemical names are

179

listed along with trademark names used in the United States so that prescriptions can be refilled with the identical compound prescribed in the United States.

Valium (diazepam) can be helpful in decreasing acute anxiety or panic. However, its effects often last many hours or days, and some people feel sleepy when they take this medication frequently.

Librium (chlordiazepoxide) is similar in effects and side effects to Valium.

Dalmane (fluorazepam) is an excellent sedative. It disturbs the rhythm of normal sleep only minimally and, therefore, is widely prescribed by physicians. However, its effects, like those of Librium and Valium, may last for many hours.

Barbiturates (Nembutal, Seconal, Amytal) induce sleep effectively and are eliminated from the body more quickly than Dalmane, Librium, or Valium. However, in contrast to Dalmane, they decrease in effectiveness if used over a number of nights. Because of this decrease in effectiveness over a period of time, some patients tend to increase medication dosage and run the risk of habituation or addiction. Many physicians no longer prescribe barbiturates because of their dangerous complications.

My recommendations for the use of sedative and tranquilizing drugs, to be checked out with your physician, are these:

No psychoactive medications should be used without regular consultations with a physician.

For sleep when traveling, or for acute sleeplessness, Nembutal in a small dose acts quickly and is eliminated quickly. Dalmane is a reliable sedative for people who are sick or have a persistent sleep problem. Benadryl is a useful sedative and, in small doses, can be used effectively with children.

Valium and Librium are effective tranquillizers in times of great stress or acute anxiety.

Help for Personal Problems

During a consultation trip in Asia, I had lunch with a young couple. As we talked in their living room, I noticed the titles of two books on a coffee table, *Up From Depression* and *Prayers for the Despondent*. When her husband left to return to his office, the woman began to pour out a story of loneliness and secret drinking throughout the day followed by a hurried attempt to put on a happy face when her children and husband returned late in the afternoon. She felt trapped and could think of no way to reach out to get help for herself.

This woman felt overwhelmed by her conviction that she could not trust anyone else to be concerned about her unhappiness. As a result, she became entangled in a downward spiral of loneliness and guilt. She was unable to respond to the basic human need to share feelings and worries, because she felt there was no one to whom she could turn.

When faced with seemingly insurmountable problems—personal misery, a delinquent child, an alcoholic husband—people feel trapped and may overlook the many opportunities available for putting problems in perspective.

Where, indeed, can a person living in a fishbowl existence overseas turn for support and wise counsel?

Look to Your Own Resources First

Put aside some time to think through a particular problem. If you write out what is bothering you, you may see the problem in sharper outline. View a situation in relationship to the requirements of your entire family (chap. 6). You may be able to identify a missing element in your life; the need for an intimate friend, a meaningful job, or an involving activity (chap. 5).

Talking

Talk, for instance, with your son who teases his brother unmercifully. Get his point of view about the issue. Try to discover what he feels he is up against. Talk with his teachers and other parents about him so that you can get as complete a view as possible of the situation.

If your spouse mopes around and leaves tasks uncompleted, set a definite, quiet time when the two of you can discuss problems. A depressed person finds it difficult to reach out and speak about troubles. A regular time put aside to talk about personal and family problems can be of immense help in resolving them.

Friendships

Friends in the community should be your first line of defense outside your family. Don't overlook the comfort you can get from sharing your concerns with someone you respect. If your ten-year-old son has been caught stealing a toy from a PX, you may feel that the child's entire future has been ruined. Someone who has been through such an experience can assure you that all children want to steal at one time or another and most do. She will remind you that an admired son of one of your friends went through such a stage and emerged as a healthy teenager, and that children typically covet possessions and don't consider it too terrible to appropriate money or a toy.

Because the people who constitute the usual first line of defense—parents, sisters, or brothers—simply are not available overseas, it is important to seek out someone in your circle with whom you can share anxieties and disappointments. Men need such intimates, too, but rarely allow themselves the luxury of seeking them. That is sad, particularly overseas, for men who are on display most of the time are unusually vulnerable to a loss of perspective about their estimation of themselves and their families.

Books

Look for relevant books that deal with your concerns. In the last few years, extremely well-written books have been published about such diverse issues as depression, sexual problems, learning difficulties in children, divorce, alcoholism, and adolescent troubles. Some people gain much understanding and support through reading about the problems they face.*

Discussion Groups

A group of people who gather together regularly can share experiences and knowledge and give one another support. Parent discussion groups that meet around such issues as child-rearing or sex education flourish in many posts. The defined topic—be it great books, Zen studies, or Transactional Analysis—may not be the most important element of the group. Rather, group members gain strength and pleasure from the shared intimacy of meeting together definite times.

If such a group does not exist in your community, and you believe the community needs greater closeness, try to organize one yourself. Search for an expert in archaeology or history who might be your leader at the start. Ask a social worker or former teacher about the possibility of guiding a group concerned with the education of your children. A teacher, coun-

---

* The Mental Health Materials Center, 419 Park Avenue South, New York, New York 10016, can refer you to helpful publications.

selor, or psychologist in your community school who has worked with groups may be able to help you get started.

In a small, intimate community there is a certain risk involved in starting a discussion group that focuses on personal concerns. Under such circumstances, it is especially important to pay careful attention to issues of confidentiality and the relevance of discussion topics. The group leader would benefit greatly from the consultation of a psychiatrist or psychologist skilled in group processes.

Many community problems can be resolved or placed in better perspective through the use of groups. Teenages benefit greatly from serious, though informal discussion of drugs or sexuality. In a troubled time, meetings to discuss fears of kidnapping or political insurrection can help to allay feelings of panic.

Naturally, each group requires planning. Teenagers want to run things themselves and do best with the concept of peer counseling. A group on a military post must take into account the built-in problems of rank and hierarchy. But such difficulties can be ironed out by willing, sensitive people. Some members of the career-overseas community have considered this area of activity to be so important that they have returned to the United States for courses in group process to prepare themselves to organize and lead a variety of group activities.

Seek original ways to increase communication about important issues. Persuade the editors of magazines or newsletters in your area of the world to introduce a column of advice or questions and answers to deal with personal and family concerns. Similar columns in U.S. newspapers are popular and seem to fill an important need. Perhaps the *Foreign Service Journal, The International Herald Tribune,* or *The Overseas American* might agree to print such a column.

When You Need Help: Medical and Personal

Ministers and Physicians

Look to the ministers and physicians in your community for personal consultation when you find that you cannot solve a problem in a reasonable period of time by the use of your own resources. Ask among your friends about which of the professionals in your community might be most responsive to your individual concerns.

In isolated areas, *specialists* from American military installations can be called on for consultation in certain cases; base hospitals can be tapped as an emergency service backup. Traveling consultants often visit such bases and, in critical situations, are happy to consult in the civilian community. During overseas trips, I have spent many hours in just such consultations.

Well-trained, English-speaking *psychiatrists and psychologists* practice in Rome, Paris, Manila, Karachi, London, Bogota, Bangkok, and many other cities. Many of these specialists were trained in fine American and British universities and hospitals. You may have to do some detective work to track down just the right person to deal with your particular problems, so be prepared to check through a number of resources—your doctor, the medical society, the psychiatric association, or the American embassy.

Remember that you can *call* a psychiatrist or counselor in the United States by overseas telephone and get an immediate consultation. If such a call is preceded by an explanatory letter, a psychiatrist often can give you a precise opinion over the phone. For a number of years, the Peace Corps used phone and mail consultation between the field and Washington, D.C., in order to resolve hundreds of medical and psychological problems.

If a family *problem persists or worsens* over a period of

time—a month or more—do not vacillate. Make it an urgent priority and get back to the United States for appropriate consultation.

Useful Books

American National Red Cross, *Standard First Aid and Personal Safety* (New York: Doubleday, 1973). Extremely helpful for emergencies and camping trips.

Carter, James P., and West, Eleanora de Antonia, *Keeping Your Family Healthy Overseas* (New York: Delacorte Press, 1971). Especially useful for families who live in hot countries because it covers snakes, insects, and diarrhea thoroughly.

Directory of the International Association of Medical Assistance to Travelers: I.A.M.A.T., Suite 5620, Empire State Building, New York, N.Y. 10001. Lists over 500 English-speaking, and predominantly American-trained, doctors, clinics, and hospitals throughout the world.

Greenberg, Henry F., ed., *Child Care* (Nutley, New Jersey: Rocom Press, Hoffmann-LaRoche Inc., 1973). Contains valuable comments on such recurrent care issues as "Respiratory Problems," "Growth and Development," and "Medication and Treatment."

Holvey, D. N., ed., *The Merck Manual of Diagnosis and Therapy* (Rahway, New Jersey: Merck, Sharp and Dohme Research Labs, 1972). A 1,700-page gem of a book, printed on thin paper and very light, filled with useful data on every conceivable aspect of medical diagnosis and care. Particularly recommended for the family that will have to be responsible for a fair amount of its medical care.

Spock, Benjamin, *Baby and Child Care* (New York: Pocket Books, 1968). The standard work on ordinary health problems of children and child development concerns.

"I should . . . like well enough to spend
the whole of my life in traveling abroad, if
I could anywhere borrow another life to
spend afterwards at home!"
—William Hazlitt

Travelers' Return: Reentry into the United States

A MOMENT will come, often without warning, when you will decide that it is time to return to the United States. The moment may surprise you as you linger over photographs of a Labor Day beach scene in *Newsweek* or *Time* during a mid-morning coffee break, or seize you when your children complain for the one hundredth time about the weather in Stockholm or Calcutta. Pay attention to changes in your attitude, for the next steps may well be fervent farewells, hurried packing, and a dash back to the United States.

Although people on short-term assignments may experience something of the drama of that moment of decision, old hands who have lived away from the United States most of their lives find that a wish to return, once aroused, can become an obses-sion that summons up a disquieting mélange of ambitions, fantasies, and uncertainties. A willingness to sort out the jum-ble of such deep-rooted, but normal concerns will aid im-measurably in the transition process to the United States. In some cases, of course, the family begins their journey home at the request of the government or a civilian employer. Many events and thoughts can set the wheels of return in motion. The following possibilities all crop up frequently:

—Children speak English with an Italian accent and use fractured metaphors—"break your bridges behind you," "life is just a bowl of nuts."

—The entire family balks at moving again. One father re-called such a time: "It is easier to travel around the globe when your children are small; then it gets more and more difficult," he recounted. "Move by move I felt more and more resistance to change from everybody in the family, until a time came when they just refused to be bounced around anymore."

—The economic advantages dissolve. "Money got us over-seas in the first place, and money is sending us back. I just couldn't pass up a good job opportunity in the States, espe-cially when the cost of living has gone up so much here," explained a businessman about to return to the United States.

—The political and social atmosphere becomes constrict-ing. A thoughtful doctor described the problem this way:

I was asked to stay in my job, but something hard to put into words made me come back to the United States. I was interested in social and political events in Africa, but had to bite my tongue about them. I couldn't fire off a letter to the newspaper if I felt that there was some injustice committed or that another point of view should be made known. You're a guest in a foreign country; you're invited to work there and it's not appropriate to say critical things even though you have strong feelings about issues. I like to live where I can say what I want and stick my neck out sometimes. When you're overseas, you always have to censor wry humor and ironic expressions. You're on guard all of the time. When all that got to me, I decided it was time to buy a ticket home.

—Conflicting ambitions and loyalties may surface. "I've been perfectly happy here," a successful businessman in Europe said, "but I think there is a much faster world around, and I want our children to have some experience with it. They really have to decide whether they are going to be Europeans or Americans, a decision my wife and I never truly faced in our own lives."

By far the most frequent reason parents cite for deciding to return stateside is the needs of their children. A mother recalled to me:

As each of our teenagers wants a summer job, which is not available here, or prepares to go off to college in the United States, we feel the tug of separation a little more. We began to think that it was time to pull up stakes here when that big ocean came between us and our children, and we realized how difficult it would be to continue to touch base with them.

Double-check your judgment, even after you have decided to return. Are you terminating your work because of a fear that a large task may be too difficult to complete? The rhythm of short-term assignments and short-term goals tends to mold singles hitters rather than home-run specialists. But, at times, home runs are possible. Are deeper uncertainties obscured by immediate concerns about children? Look into all possible motivations before you make an irrevocable decision, for a second look may result in a renewed commitment to a job and a country. That silent voice saying, "Maybe we should stay one more year, always one more year," may reflect an inner truth.

Once you have decided to return, the chain of circumstances set in motion should be permitted to continue. Keep to the sequence of decision and action, followed by a determined withdrawal of involvement from your overseas country. It may be painful to leave, and some sudden doubts make one question the decision many times. At this point, one might remember the words of Satchel Paige: "Don't look back; something may be catching up on you."

Authorities always suggest total openness with one's family as one ponders a return. This includes talking with everyone about the reasons involved in a decision to return; far more problems arise from what is left out of discussions than from what is included. A father might share his hopes for career advancement that motivate a return to the home office of his company. Candor demands that the father place all the facts on the table. Yes, the challenge of his overseas work has disappeared, if that is a consideration, or yes, the salary increase at headquarters can't be overlooked.

"We are going home because of you," is a statement and accusation sometimes made to a child that often veils a father's boredom with his work or a mother's dissatisfaction because of lack of career opportunities. Such a statement will fool nobody but confuse everyone. On the other hand, be frank if a child's adjustment problems motivate a return to the United States. To pull out of an emotional nosedive, a child may indeed be better off with the security of his home town or a special school. If that is the case, his parents can convey a positive stand rather than a punitive one by saying: "We want to go home so that you will have a chance to catch up in school and feel good about yourself." No guilt, no criticism, no deception need be involved.

Families are often surprised to find themselves sad when they expected to be delighted by the anticipation of going home to the U.S. Such sadness, a kind of "going home blues," is natural enough; it hits when one considers all the friends never to be seen again, the abandoned adventures, the uncertainty of returning to a changed United States. One person recalled, "Travel means disruption to me. We were always leaving some place forever, and I always felt bad about leaving friends among the local people because I knew our paths would never cross again." Moves generate varying amounts of turmoil depending upon the previous life experiences of a person, the number and kinds of losses he has sustained in his life, and the pleasure with which he anticipates the present move. Some disturbance, if not prolonged, is a normal part of any important move and must be accepted.

Parents and children who have thrived on a highly visible, significant overseas existence may feel a letdown when they return to the crowded anonymity of a city such as Washington, D.C. When a father's work no longer affects global politics or even his neighbors in the next office, when a mother must settle for supermarkets instead of *souks*, and children for baseball instead of snake charmers, discouragement may set in. At such a time, parents need to work especially hard to balance the uncertainty involved in a return to the United States with a recognition and participation in the great satisfactions available here. Though exotic experiences may be difficult to find in Washington, substitutions and new activities can be sought out.

Not everyone dreads moving. Some people enjoy the continual change woven into overseas life. For those happy nomads, moving is easy. A Foreign Service officer stated it this way:

Once the habit of moving gets into your blood, you always itch for the next challenge. I love the contrast in work from one country to another. When I go back to New York and see my friends doing the same things they have always done, it depresses me. I really thrive on getting a new pack of cards every four years; you're not stuck with anything, and when you finish a job you just close your desk on it and go off to a new one.

Leave-taking

Let us now look at the painful part of leave-taking, for the joyous side—the presents, toasts, address exchanges, and plans to meet again—is easy to accept. Though a man may shut his desk joyfully on mistakes when he leaves a country, he also closes doors on friendships and must distract himself from the mountains not climbed, the shrines not visited. There is no second chance, no second act in overseas experience. The French proverb says it well: *Partir c'est mourir un peu.* ("To part is to die a little.")

In the United States, we rarely part from friends forever, but the overseas family must say final good-byes repeatedly. Many families who found the experience an increasingly wrenching one slip into an unfortunate habit of evading the farewells and good-byes. There is no lack of parties to celebrate leave-taking and, in fact, a last month at a post can be lost in a blur of good-bye parties. But parties only obscure rather than cure the pain of leave-taking. Though an effective short-term narcotic, they can be a very expensive one because they don't leave much time to pack and close up an overseas life. Experienced travelers ration the amount of partying they do and, instead, concentrate on the important tasks of leaving.

Find a way to arrange small gatherings with your closest host country friends and colleagues. Identify friends who can be part of a supporting system for you, the "intimates" described in chapter 4, "The Art of Transition." Speak openly with them about the feelings that arise as you leave them. Take the time to put together the past, the present, and the future as you talk with them. People who gloss over good-byes and forget to see friends, or omit that final handshake or embrace for fear of crying, often find that they carry with them a legacy of disturbance or guilty sadness.

Travelers' Return: Reentry into the United States

Make a Checklist of Your Requirements and Wishes

Do you want to continue to live in the town you left? Will you return to your previous career? Will your friends be waiting for you or will they have taken on other interests and activities that will no longer include you?

Since mobility is such an important part of contemporary life, many people seriously consider geography, climate, and outdoor interests when they decide where they want to live. Remember the truth that "you can't go home again." An American must take into account the years he has been away, the changes that occurred in his local situation, and the transformations he has gone through in his life. Few people are satisfied to return to an old job and an old neighborhood.

Explore new possibilities through the help of friends, overseas contacts, and employment agencies. Attend national and international business meetings or conventions in your field; travel within the United States when you return, if you can possibly arrange to do so. Most people can settle on a job and a place to live with little trouble if the personal dimensions of their lives are in good order. Therefore, the next sections will explore personal dimensions of leave-taking and homecoming.

Caretakers

"You can go back to Boston, but I'm staying in Rio with Nina, and that's that," a young girl declared to her parents as they prepared to return to the United States, and she seriously meant what she said. For five years Nina, the family housekeeper, had been part of this young girl's everyday life. Nina picked out clothes, cooked the meals, played with the youngster, and filled her with the tales, sayings, and folklore of Brazil. The mother had precipitately announced—not without some relief at the thought of separating her daughter from the housekeeper—that their family was to return to the United States without Nina. The child's complaint was entirely reasonable under those circumstances.

Everyone in a family becomes attached to the staff, even to cleaning women who may come in only once a week. In many families, it is the maids with whom both parents and children share delights, confide secrets, or mourn their failures. Because of the amount of time a child spends with a caretaker and his great need for someone to depend upon, he may give his loyalty to her and, in the process, become alienated from his mother. The result will be pandemonium at the time of departure.

Maids who become part of the family deserve as much attention and concern as any other family member. Unfortunately, everyone's feelings tend to be slighted in a move, and people who move frequently may become insensitive to the strong attachments they and their children form with servants. Though insensitivity usually is a defense against facing the pain of leaving a cherished friend, it is not a very effective one.

Leave-taking, the good, the bad, and the sad, should be shared with the servants. In any case, there is no way to hide the clues of moving. When torn linen is not replaced or a mother lets a statement slip about "putting away the winter clothes because we won't be here next year" or clothes and toys are shipped back to the United States, everyone knows that something is up. It is healthiest to say something like this to a child's caretaker:

> We have orders to go back to the United States in June. You have been wonderful with our daughter and our whole family, and we

> so appreciate the love and kindness you have shown. It is going to
> be tough on all of us from now on until we leave, and I know we
> won't be able to help feeling sad sometimes. But we will all work
> together, and we will certainly help you in any way we can to get
> another job after we leave. (No half promises of taking her to the
> United States, no teasing about the possibility that you might stay
> longer.)

And to your child:

> We know you love Nina very much and so do we, but we are
> going back to the United States because your father has a better
> job there. Nina will stay here because this is her country and the
> place where she is most comfortable. I know you may feel sad and
> even angry about this, and you can talk about your feelings. We
> will keep in touch with Nina and we know that she will be very
> proud of how well you keep growing up.

What other possibilities are there to soften the inevitable
blow? Talk about departure with your family and with your
close friends well ahead of the time you leave, perhaps a
month or more. Reassure young children, who worry about
whether they will be cared for and cherished, that "we are
going home to the United States, where I will take care of you
even more than I have here, but your nanny will stay in her
own country."

Talk through and be willing to live through a certain
amount of disturbance that everyone will feel. Don't try to
combat the pain and don't fight it with anger, irritability, or
complaints; you will have enough of that from your children.
Rather, live with the disturbance awhile, for it will eventually
wear away and children will begin to look to the future with
happiness. It simply takes "psychological" time to disengage
from important experiences.

Don't abandon your children to servants in the first place.
Retain responsibility for a significant part of their lives wherever you are.

If you are considering bringing any members of your household staff with you to the United States, note that although this is an unusual plan, it can sometimes work out well for all: but make sure such a plan is not a way to avoid the pain of separation. Don't assume that maids who adapt well to your life in Italy will make the transition to the alien environment of the United States comfortably. Some maids or nurses, like some wines, do not travel well. And, be very wary of bringing the children of your servants to the United States with you. You may also bring big transcultural headaches for them and yourself.

Relatives

Relatives may well view the return of traveling family members with a mixture of joy, possessiveness, and envy. Brace yourself for a complicated reception from your cousins and brothers. One mother recalled:

> You come back and face a concentrated dose of family problems—my sister's divorce, our father's dislike of his nursing home—and you wish you had remained overseas. Our children are strangers to their grandparents. They really don't know their cousins or their peers in the United States. The children, especially small children, are expected to just love their grandparents, and, when they don't, grandparents can react critically. The whole homecoming thing can go up in smoke before your eyes.

Be prepared for that "concentrated dose of family problems" by corresponding with your family while you work overseas. Participate in family decisions by mail. Keep your oar in even when your overseas situation might be a convenient excuse for disregarding family responsibilities.

Many returning families have learned to focus a reunion

with relatives around a birthday or anniversary. Some families have found it helpful to settle down somewhere during a prolonged home leave and invite relatives to visit them for short periods of time.

Although relatives and friends may profess a great interest in your overseas adventures, their attention span is short for exotic reports. They return quickly to a preoccupation with gardens, money, gossip, and personal troubles. Overseas life offers a freedom from such preoccupations, but it is an unnatural freedom, rarely sustained on the return home. Most people feel that it is best simply to dig in and talk about the gardens, family complications, and high prices, for the best way to overcome small talk is to give in to it a little. Ties, roots, and a sense of identity consist to a great extent of an immersion in the daily lives of the people around us, an immersion that can be too easily avoided by families who live overseas. Families who follow the maxim that "life is daily" have little trouble finding a comfortable place in the United States.

Men

The entire process of anticipation, transition, and settling in gets replayed when you return home, but in reverse and with an important difference. Instead of the anticipation of adventure and ample time to be with his family, a man's arrival in the United States may signal a return to narrowed career interests and less time for a family to be together.

A husband may catch himself day-dreaming about the amenities of his office back in London, of tea breaks and spirited discussions at lunch in pleasant clubs. Even though life in London does not consist solely of international deals consummated over club lunches, his recollection, like the rosy recollections of adolescence, can make it seem that way. He may be rudely awakened to discover that he has lost ground with colleagues in his field who have continued to keep abreast of developments while he was isolated from sources of new knowledge. Disillusionment can set in unless the importance of an overseas experience is put into perspective.

The stateside return offers an opportunity for careful selection of realistic goals, a chance to focus on what one really wants to accomplish in a career, a hobby, or within the family, free of the continual uncertainty that is built into overseas living. The move home to Chicago can become an opportunity to test new interests and priorities formulated in the relative isolation of overseas living, as a person makes job contacts and searches for challenging career opportunities. Many men have concluded that the lesson of overseas experience has been that they have gained through it the freedom to mold their careers independently of what they believed was expected of them.

Women

Women who go back to a customary way of life readjust to the United States more readily than their husbands. A mother can organize her days as she wishes without regard to the schedule of the head of her husband's company or agency. The familiarity of relatives, friends, and activities can do a great deal to cushion the transition. The overseas role of sharing in a husband's career on a party circuit each night disappears, but so do the obligatory parties at which the same faces appear night after night. The sense of participation in international politics vanishes, but so does the tedious repetition of superficial generalizations and guarded statements.

Travelers' Return: Reentry into the United States

Housekeepers disappear, too, and, as one mother said, "I just put my diploma up over my washing machine and started back to work." Even mothers who have employed servants minimally overseas will notice an altered tempo when children have to be driven to school and to scout meetings and meals must be prepared three times a day with no backup from an American club.

It is true, of course, that some people become returnees by choice while others go back at the request of the government or civilian employers. Both these groups have something in common, though.

"Overseas you gear your life to other people, your maids, your husband, and the children," a mother recalled. "Here you can decide what you want to do and begin to choose a career." Many women echo this sentiment. But the time to plan a graduate school course or new job is when you are still overseas so that you can begin to put out feelers before you have gotten back to your home.

In the last several years, women's liberation and feminist groups have powerfully influenced thinking about the role of women in the United States. Any returning women should follow the ideas of these groups so that new opportunities can be considered.

More Hints for Returning Men and Women

Husbands and wives might choose to plan together for their lives on return. After a period overseas, goals change, new career interests develop, priorities shift. A man may decide to settle on a less demanding job in order to help with his children and allow his wife to work in a career that will fulfill her needs best. A women might reassess the financial needs of her family in the light of changed priorities developed overseas. When you return, take into account the availability of, for example, a large kiln for potters, a graduate school relevant to the wishes of a husband or wife, and recreation facilities for those who have learned to love particular aspects of nature.

Consider a new career or a modification in an old one when you return. No matter how interesting or remunerative the job you left in the United States may have been, it will seem pallid upon your return, for needs change, experience broadens, and growth occurs during an overseas tour. Even a small change from a previous job pattern will help in reintegration. Most old hands counsel that it is better to return to no job at all than to sink back into the exact routine that had been left.

Reintegration takes time, often a year or more, and it requires effort and planning. Be certain that your company knows in detail what you did overseas. Present these experiences and write about them; volunteer to develop an international club in your organization or an international branch of your work. Keep in touch with your company while you are away, even if it isn't necessary, so that your colleagues will know what you have been doing and can prepare for your return in a way that will help you fit in well. Expect that you will feel uncertain, uncomfortable, and perhaps even unwanted within your firm for a while. Give yourself and your colleagues time to reintegrate your return to the United States.

What you have learned and absorbed overseas becomes part of you; you cannot repudiate an important block of life experience, even though, as one returned traveler noted, "You just cannot truly communicate with others who have not traveled and so you just learn not to be disappointed when you meet with resistance or indifference from your friends."

Many people combine overseas life and the United States by participation in an international organization such as the Circolo Italiano, the Alliance Française, foreign relations committees, the Asia Society, or similar organizations that exist in many large cities. If organizations congenial to your interests do not exist in your city, consider starting one, since this is a sure way to find others who share your interests. The opportunity to entertain foreign students and visiting professionals from other countries, and to introduce these visitors to American friends, can be most stimulating.

If living abroad has changed your priorities, and you no longer are willing to spend your time doing housework, chauffeuring children, or mowing the lawn, it may be possible to free yourself of some of these chores. Establish car pools; give your children responsibilities for meals and caring for a part of your house; have everyone share in the chores of the house. Take charge of your life when you return by making a list of the irreducible minimum of work to be done and distribute that work among your family. Disabuse yourself of the idea that there are mother's chores, father's responsibilities, and children's messiness. Don't get locked into a schedule that is imposed by a child's music lessons, a husband's breakfast, a woman's bridge group. Look for new friends and new opportunities that fit your altered wishes.

List the differences in the use of time between your life in Caracas, Venezuela, and in Indianapolis, Indiana; chart the hours from morning to night and from Sunday to Sunday. What of your overseas life can be transferred to the United States and what will not travel? How can you adapt to the tempo of commuting, car pools, distant jobs? How do you fill the vacuum left when there are no caretakers, baby-sitters, or instant playmates?

Learn the new words and phrases that have crept into American speech just as seriously as you would set yourself the task of learning another foreign language. Read American magazines, watch television as an educational chore, and take time to talk with children you come in contact with at playgrounds or schools.

Retain control of your children. If you want them to play with a particular group of friends, seek out congenial families;

join a church or social club that fits your views. Be certain to talk about your values with your children. Constrast your values, if necessary, with the street or school values children encounter. Be sure to discuss your views about drugs, dating hours, sexuality, and the use of cars.

Be yourself. If you have learned to like espresso, buy an espresso machine. But don't try to keep up and fit in at any cost, or you may repeat the experience of one returnee who said:

> The first year home we bought an expensive barbecue grill, grilled steaks every night, and dressed in "mod" clothes. It was ridiculous. Then we began to realize that we didn't need to have a color TV or sugar-coated cereal every morning, even though our children sometimes fought for those very things. My husband and I realize that we learned some things overseas and decided to keep those things we had learned for ourselves and our children.

Turn invidious comparisons you might be tempted to make to good use. When you recall with a sigh that "in Bogota we always enjoyed a three-hour lunch together," consider ways in which you might make the day in the United States more pleasing with an occasional long lunch or a special outing.

A particularly thoughtful adult summed up his philosophy of return this way:

> When you get back, you can't expect people to want to hear about your travels, but you do bring things that people need—the sense of community you notice in small towns in Greece; the humane way people deal with each other in villages; the slow pace of people who take time to be with each other.

The traveler is not everyman. He is unusual because he decided to leave the United States, and, when he comes back, he will necessarily have different expectations from the person who has always lived here. His expectations can be put to use but should not be imposed upon his new neighbors.

Children

To give some flavor of the repatriation impact on children, let us look at a potpourri of reactions expressed on the subject.

—"Everyone expects you to be a real freak. They shake your hand and look at you like you're a specimen or something. When you tell them you're from Thailand, they say, 'Oh, what part of Texas is that?' "

> We guarded and controlled the lives of our children overseas; their friends were the children of our friends. Now that we are back in the United States we say, "Gee kids, you are back home now. Go to it. There's nothing to be afraid of," and we just toss them off. When we told our thirteen-year-old to make friends on her own at school, she whirled on us and said, "When are you and Daddy going to realize it isn't that easy? Foreigners may be flattered when we introduce ourselves and ask their names and show some curiosity about the ways of their countries, but here they make fun of me when I ask questions because I am supposed to be one of them!"

This mother concluded her views with this bit of advice, "Coming home is really much more difficult than going abroad, and parents have to be far more understanding of the problems their children face when they come home."

> I was really excited to go home, but I hated my first day in school here. My junior high school graduating class in Saudi Arabia had just fifteen other kids. This high school has 2,000 kids and it is unbelievable. You even have to get a pass to go to the john. The school is filled with cliques, the kids who do dope, the cheerleaders, the sports kids. I just couldn't get in with any of them; I didn't like them and they didn't like me. I felt I was more mature than the other kids, and the things they thought were important seemed trivial to me. "What am I going to wear to school today?" "Who am I going to walk home with?" Those are just not big things in my life. I was afraid of these kids because, even though I felt more mature, they knew a lot more about living in America than I did.

The attitudes of parents make an immense difference in how their children settle in. Here are some ways in which parents have helped children find a place when they return to the United States:

We were able to rent a house next door to a playground and moved in two months before school started. It was marvelous for our children to be able to walk out the door freely, ride their bikes anywhere, and go to the corner drugstore without having to check in, after being in the Middle East, where these freedoms were not possible. We helped our thirteen-year-old get into the Boy Scouts through a talk with the boy who delivered newspapers. My daughter immediately looked for a place to rent a horse and found friends around the stables. We joined a community swimming pool, where our children made lots of friends. Our kids didn't have any real problems of reentry into the United States, but it is something you have to work at; it doesn't just happen. Our thirteen-year-old is in a huge junior high school, which is quite a change for him, but I just told him that I knew he could make a place for himself, and he has.

We all looked forward to coming back to New Jersey. Then when we got here, the first thing we faced was a real crush on a bus. Everyone was jammed in and elbowed each other; nobody was friendly. In fact, Americans in general aren't friendly. I looked at my son and both of us said, "What did we come home for?" So we just talked it out and decided the only way to make friends was to be friendly no matter what happened, and it worked.

Other parents have offered different advice from their experience in reintegrating their children into community life in the United States:

Bring back as many of a child's treasures as you can stuff into a trunk—his books, banners, swords, rocks, shards, and resign yourself to the extra freight costs. You will be packing an important part of your child's security, and he will need that security when he first returns to the United States.

Do your best to make the first day in a new home a pleasant one. Explore the neighborhood you live in, its back streets and markets as well as its monuments and shopping centers. Arrange for a visit with friends around baseball, soccer, or a picnic. Give your children and yourself a total immersion experience in your new country.

Children change, parents change, all of life changes when you return home. Children's reactions will be variable, so caution them to expect jolts, for they will encounter some. Prepare your children to absorb novel experiences and show them the same example of positive anticipation you recall from the time you first went overseas.

Schools

As in moving overseas, a youngster returning home needs some help in finding his way in an American school. Ideally, on the first day a child sets foot in school, he should know how to play baseball, football, soccer, basketball, and hockey; he should know the names of outstanding professional and college stars in each of these sports and the standings of teams in his city. He should also know the current movie stars, TV actors, rock groups, and advertising slogans. It would help if he could speak in the current slang and wear clothes indistinguishable from those of all the other children in his class. This may seem a rather odd, even preposterous, educational prescription, but children do well in their classrooms when their personal lives are serene, and they feel best if they feel "in." Education prepares children to adjust in society and only secondarily to become scholars. You can help your child "break in" more easily with his peers in a new school if you alert him to at least some of the items in the long list enumerated above.

Most children want to be as ordinary as possible in a new

school, to slip in unobstrusively and find their way. Teachers with a misdirected sense of kindness will interfere by immediately introducing new children from overseas to other children from abroad—the English or Brazilian child in a class, rather than the one from Iowa. This segregates the youngster from others in his environment just as surely as the golden ghetto separates families from host country nationals overseas. A timely word to a teacher or principal can help block a natural tendency to introduce foreigner to foreigner. Similarly, children should be steered away from international clubs and teachers should be discouraged from asking your child to speak on Kuwait and the oil issue at an assembly.

Although any sensible mother will be certain not to dress up her child in a dashiki, Eton collar, or sarong on the first day of school, there are lots of variations on this theme unwittingly perpetrated by parents. Block the impulses to dress a child in a unique way. Children appreciate the blessed anonymity of looking exactly like everyone else in their class.

What children speak of as the "violence" of American schools can be the most difficult thing for them to get used to. As one thirteen-year-old recalled:

> I had been taught to have a lot of respect for my elders, my teachers, and the other kids. When I came back to the United States, I couldn't understand how people could yell at each other in the way they did. I would never have thumbed my nose at a teacher in Africa, said nasty things about him behind his back, switched books on him, or knocked over chairs in a classroom. But just those things happened during my first year in junior high school here. Sure we had wrestling matches and sometimes we would throw mangos at each other in Africa, but things never got to a point where you were actually beating someone up.

Another recently returned child noted: "Cheating just didn't exist in Ethiopia. The teachers would give you a test, put it on your desk, and then leave. Here, cheating was the thing, and I just didn't know what to do because I had never seen it happen before."

A pecking order is a reality, as is a certain amount of hazing. A teenager needs to be able to roll with the punches when people blame him for the troubles in the Middle East or call him "Frenchie" even though he is entirely American.

Dating patterns can throw some returnees for a loss. Here is one fourteen-year-old's view of it?

> I had been given definite lines of right and wrong when I was overseas, so when I came to junior high school in the United States, I found I had to make decisions like a much older kid—decisions about dancing, staying out late, being in the company of one fellow alone. I came to a school where drugs and smoking were in things, and booze was sneaked into school.

Before you return to the United States, you might take a deep breath and talk plainly with a child, boy or girl, about petting and sexuality, the handling of drinking, and drug use. Families need to reestablish their views about codes of behavior and expectations of their children. Children who have never been exposed to such experiences need clear statements from their parents. You can't depend upon a child in transition, who is highly vulnerable to peer group pressures, to make decisions for himself without any preparation.

Adolescents

Settling in is particularly difficult for teenagers, because the high-school culture puts a premium on excluding unusual people (chap. 10). Parents can help by seeking other families with high-school-age children and letting the children get together before the beginning of a term. Family outings, picnics, a community swimming pool, or church activity can be a natural way for children to discover what is expected of them and then share their views with their parents.

Although the line between over-protectiveness and social independence is a fine one, parents will best help by being perhaps a bit more intrusive into a child's life than they might choose to be. You cannot depend totally upon your child's previous upbringing to help him make decisions. Try to be available to discuss the issues he will face and give him extra help if he has trouble adjusting to a school. Passivity on the part of parents breeds unhappiness, isolation, or unfortunate involvements in their youngsters. Teenagers need all the help they can get in order to find the friends they need so much; parents perform an invaluable service if they can identify those first acquaintances that often blossom into friends.

A child returning from overseas must submerge most of his foreign experiences and become a kind of "double" person. One adolescent put it this way:

> You end up with a double concept of yourself. There is this sense that you have an extra talent, your knowledge of another language and another culture, that has no value except in planning your own later life. I think where people get in trouble is that they tend to come back and know they have this asset, but think that everybody else should know about it and feel "you should respect me because I've got this extra experience," but it doesn't apply. What you gain from experience abroad is going to be maintained, but it's better to tuck it away. What you have learned not only doesn't get you anywhere but it tends to threaten or irritate people.

Accept the fact that, as one teenager put it, "People don't like to hear about foreign places that much." Americans, like all nationals, hardly appreciate criticism of the United States from those who haven't lived here for years. Despite the fact that we have many reasons to be critical of ourselves, American teenagers who complain about race relations, drugs, or whatever they are upset about merely alienate themselves from their peers. Teenagers learn to be tactful about issues if they see tact utilized at home. As a teenager commented, "When you hear your parents run down everything about the United States or yearn endlessly for another culture, some of those views rub off on you."

Loneliness

Most teenagers have been shielded from loss by the strength of their ties to their parents; many of them have never been plunged into the sadness that comes from the awareness that nothing can truly replace an important loss. The return to the United States can trigger a first recognition of loneliness in a young person, particularly when he has left best friends and finds none to take their place. When the peer group excludes him or makes unacceptable demands for entrance, an adolescent will have to decide how he will handle the inevitable isolation that ensues, for his overseas experiences will not fit easily into a high school in Philadelphia or a college in Boulder. Fortunately, youngsters can learn to cope with their temporary status of being "outsiders." Once they accept occasional loneliness as an inevitable aspect of life rather than an avoidable curse, they can begin to move out into satisfying directions. It doesn't help to question the basis of one's loneliness, and obsessively blaming oneself for it is of no value. It is simply a natural result of leaving friends and giving up a happy way of life.

Loneliness is merely a symptom, not the whole problem. What one does with loneliness can be a problem or a challenge, an opportunity to seek within yourself your own deepest interests. Many young people overcome loneliness by immersing themselves in solitary interests such as painting, writing, reading, or the pursuit of a particular subject until they become expert in that subject. Any kind of hobby or activity can help to build a sense of one's own strength and direction. A young person should be told that loneliness isn't a problem unique to adolescents; it applies to adults as well.

The person who can identify a feeling of loneliness in himself and tolerate it as a normal, though painful phenomenon that occurs when important relationships are lost and new ones not yet found can gain strength from the experience and become a uniquely stronger individual.

A Love Affair with a Foreign Way of Life

A wise host country teacher alerted me to a poignant element of life overseas. He said:

> American teenagers who come to our school develop strong attachments and sometimes intense crushes with Italian youngsters. They become inseparable, for each sees in the other, at a time when both are bursting with vitality, an opportunity to fulfill all of life's wishes. The breaking off of these friendships when the American goes home can be devastating for the visitor and the Italian child alike. Both suffer the effects of separation, as I know from conversations and letters, for such a long time.

A teenager often remembers such an experience as a time of having fallen in love, not only with a boyfriend or a girlfriend or a culture. The experience is remembered as a special love affair with a foreign way of life that remains in his memory as an ideal time, the first time that he did anything free of his parents. The time is remembered without any recollections of the troublesome, ordinary, or unsatisfying parts.

Some young people who have been through such an experience find themselves unable to become involved with a new school or new friends on their return to the United States. They make heavy demands upon teachers and friends, demands that often cannot be met no matter how pleasing the new persons want to be, because the teenager is yearning for an ideal person, an ideal time, that probably never did exist. He becomes convinced that things will never be as good as they were in Rome or Paris or Manila, and the feelings of loss and idealization develop into a kind of nostalgia for the great and lost past. Sometimes this nostalgia takes on the proportions of a true disease, a yearning and grieving that he thinks will never end.

One teenager who found it exceedingly difficult to adjust to surburban high-school living complained that teachers were not talking about significant things, that life was not important in the United States. In a letter to friends still in Tunisia she wrote:

> This city is about as middle-class as it can be. Our school is gigantic, made up of commuters and freaks, with no sense of spirit and a lot of people just trying to get it over with. It's tough to rise above the general sense of apathy. I sit here with your yearbook and am so envious of all of you there in Tunisia and think of how lucky you are to be isolated from the mass education we have here in the homeland.

A person dwells on the past when present satisfactions are not available. Memory sharpens the joys and smooths over the discomforts and uncertainties of a phase of life that cannot be recaptured. The past is recalled as a fairytale in which Snow White and Prince Charming cling to each other perpetually as if in a timeless moment of love. The long wait for Prince Charming is forgotten, and the question of what the two will do after their embrace is not considered.

This heightening or idealization of memory occurs because it is in the nature of things to want to ignore unpleasant reality—the discomforts and uncertainties of the past—and to recall only the blissful fulfillments. A preoccupation with nostalgia helps to put off present frustrations and the efforts necessary to become part of a new life.

Fortunately, there is a treatment for this nostalgia, a healthy injection of reality. A teenager who yearns for the skiing weekends in Japan that cannot be repeated in Kansas, or camel caravans that do not exist in New York State, needs help to become aware that the past was not all that perfect. Parents must engage in a certain amount of gentle shattering of recollections and help their children remember accurately what life had been like, not what they would like it to have been. Then, eyes and minds must be turned resolutely to the present. The procedure may be painful to all involved, but it can be exceedingly helpful.

Adults, too, sometimes need treatment for nostalgia. Fortunate ones, like this world traveler, get the assistance they need from concerned friends. A young lawyer recalled:

> For three months after I got back to the States, I just rushed around and complained about everything American. At lunch one day, a friend of my father's told me point blank, "Stop living in the past." Suddenly, I realized I had been spending all of my time here sucking my thumb and acting like an idiot. The realization hit me like a ton of bricks, and the very next morning I went downtown and got a job. After that most of the trouble was over.

The Question of Roots

All parents ask themselves similar questions about their children's future: What careers will they choose? Who will they marry? Where will they settle down? But the answers are less clear in the case of overseas children because they have ventured far out of the ordinary paths of childhood and adolescence. Puzzling over roots and identity can become an obsession, consuming time that might be used better in other pursuits, for no one knows precisely how the lives of overseas children turn out, just as we cannot forcast the future of a youngster raised in the United States with any accuracy. However, these statements from a diverse group of young people who grew up overseas give some clues and suggestions about who they are and where they are going:

—"I just think of myself as belonging to the world; not any one place, not Pennsylvania, but anywhere I can do what I want to do. I doubt if I will ever settle down or if I will ever need to."

—"I want to belong to a creative and open-minded group of people who are interested and concerned about the world. Everywhere I stay is home because I don't need a single home, just a sense of a place where my family lives."

I have lived in Italy most of my life, but I feel terribly alienated at times. It's a feeling that you don't belong anywhere, that something special has happened to you and you don't fit in or even want to fit in. Partly it's because no matter how long you are here or how well you speak the language, you're never totally accepted. You're always called a stranger. It makes me acutely aware that I have this gypsy thing inside me and no matter how long I stay here or how many countries I see, I can never satisfy the longing.

—"I don't think I could consider myself an American because I've seen too many of them. Here [in Europe] I am an American; in the States I wouldn't be."

—"Overseas people find themselves either totally unconcerned about their roots, their background, or they think about it all the time."

We had a saying in our family that home is where you hang your toothbrush. That has been enough for us. My family is home, not for the security of having a house or place to go to but just the security of relating to people that know you and care about you. It sort of isolates you from other people because no one else can possibly have shared your experience. But it makes our family

213

closer because there is a comfort in having someone around who knows you and can give you some feedback on your ideas.

The general moral of these statements may be that, if a young person has grown up overseas and knows that his parents had fulfilling overseas lives, his most natural wish would be to follow in their footsteps or carve larger footsteps. I once put the question of where overseas children would live to a mother whose career had spanned continents, revolutions, and acquaintances with heads of state. This is what she said of her children:

Two of them work overseas, one in the Foreign Service and one in business. Both will probably travel all of their lives. The third, who shared exactly the same experiences as his brothers, said that as soon as he was old enough to think about it he wanted to settle down and practice law in a small town, and live in a three-story house with an attic and just stuff that attic with things he could retrieve whenever he needed them. He said he was never going to move again, and he and his wife have stuck to that decision.

These statistics, like the statement that "All Indians walk single file; at least the two I saw did!" are not the most reliable. However, in the absence of firmer ones, the generalization that two-thirds of overseas children return overseas fits with the views of most people who have observed international families.

Children who have grown up overseas regularly gravitate to international friends and overseas careers simply because that is the world they know. Any parents who hope to direct their youngster toward a rural adult life in Middle America have taken on a large job. One couple attempted to do this when they retired from a long overseas career to a house they had owned for many years in Arkansas. Naively, they expected their daughter to be happy at the University of Arkansas, despite the fact that she had grown up in Moscow and Paris. The daughter worked herself up into what she described as a "major nervous breakdown" before she was able to recognize how important it was to move away from that setting to a more congenial one.

Young Americans who grow up overseas seem to find their roots primarily within their own families and their personal interests rather than in the attraction of a particular geographical location. They possess a stability of great strength and importance if they can find people who share the stability of interest and culture rather than place. If anything, they have a great advantage over their peers who grew up in the United States. As one college student put it:

> One of the things people have told me many times is that they thought I was more mature, more poised than most of my friends. I think that is because people who grow up overseas always experience a larger life and a more exciting one. They can turn their attention to things other than fads and popularity with the gang. They come back into the United States with assets that last all their lives.

An entire American satellite society, a "third culture" of international families who share career and personal interests in politics, humanitarian deeds, and global economics, exists in many cities around the world. Overseas children slip into this third culture naturally at this historical moment of expanding international career opportunities for Americans. Third culture people find their roots not in a neighborhood in Washington, D.C. or London but in the international community that travels around the world and discovers meaning in shared interests instead of a plot of land or an accident of geography. This large and expanding world of the third culture, combining the strength of international identity with the freedom and openness that develop from contact with varying ideologies, is the natural home of many people who have lived and worked overseas.

INDEX

Index

Index

and, 124; clubs for, 132; dating by, 125; family life and, 128-129; father's work and, 129-130; friends, making new, 126-127; hang-outs of, 124; high profile of, 124-125; high school in the United States, taking teenagers out of, 5-6; jobs for, 125-126, 131; outside activities and, 130-131; return to the United States and, 11, 132-133, 207-212; romance and, 130; school and, 9-10, 116-117, 126-129, 146-147; sexuality and, 123, 125; street relationships and, 48-49

Thailand, 95-96

Tipping, 27

Toddlers, 74-76

Toothaches, 177

Toys, 24; for one-to-three-year-olds, 75-76

Tranquilizers, 179-180

Transition to a new country, 29-45; change, need for, 44-45; city vs. country living, 33; close friends and, 38-40; competence, feeling of, 42-43; crises, 35-36, 54; disappointments, 35; emergencies, help in, 41-42; family life and, 59-62; first month abroad, 34-35; goals during, 43; hotel life and, 31-32; *pension*, living in a, 32; resources in the community and, 40-41; social isolation and, 37; welcoming ceremony, 30-31

Traveling overseas, 20-28; fears about, 22-23; luggage, 24; money worries in, 27; planning, 20-21; preparation for, 27-28; separation and loss, feelings of, 21-23; timing, 24-25; what to take along, 24-26; who should go first, 26

Twain, Mark, 15

Ullman, James R., 15

Vaccination, 159

Valium, 180

Violence, street, 49

Washing hands, 166, 168

Water, 167, 168

Work: for teenagers, 125-126, 131; teenagers and father's, 129-130